Country Parks

Edited by
Luis Paulo Faria Ribeiro

images
Publishing

Preface

Luis Paulo Faria Ribeiro
Landscape Architect, PhD, UMASS
Co-founder of Topiaris Landscape Architecture
Professor at Lisbon University

In today's world, park designs are among some of most significant expressions of contemporary art. The diversity of park design is the result of art and garden-art evolution, the changing use of public spaces, and of the deep awareness required for sustainable use of the world's natural resources. Contemporary parks are, for that reason, examples of public art, as well as examples of the belief that it is possible to reconcile land use for human activities with nature conservation and sustainable management of natural resources.

For this book, a significant number of examples of contemporary parks were selected for their significance in ecology, culture, and art. This selection enables us to better understand the diversity and the multi-purpose nature of these public spaces within their natural and cultural dimensions. Through analysis and critique, it is possible to understand how they significantly contribute to the beauty and environment of today's landscapes in rural, urban, and metropolitan settings.

In fact, the study of landscape offers an amazing history of the continuing change of land uses, originated by human influence upon natural ecosystems into ever-changing and more or less complex cultural systems. As in the words of the Portuguese landscape architect Ribeiro Telles[1], landscape should be considered the quintessence of human culture. In this sense, I would further add that parks and gardens are among the ultimate social and artistic expressions that can be found of cultural landscapes.

Gardens and parks, being cultural landscape entities, are the result of the transformation of land and resources for human activities to improve people's well-being. The first great human transformation of the land and its natural ecosystems was the establishment of clearings inside woodlands and other pristine lands, for human settlement, including pasture and agriculture. Such settlements, together with human land patterns, became the very first cultural territories, hence landscapes. The earlier transformation of the land and the perceptions of its functions to support human communities' survival can be considered the starting point of the concept of Paradise: land that could support all human needs, though in a context of pleasure, or even spirituality, without too much concern for its management. Such a concept inspired the ideal of the Arcadian landscape: an imaginary place offering peace and simplicity, and assuring survival, safety, and pleasure.

The surplus production associated with the early forms of settled agriculture 12,000 years ago, and the control of water with the first irrigation networks 6000 years ago, led eventually to the intensification of trade and wealth. This crucial moment is a consequence of the Neolithic agricultural revolution, and allowed communities to start using part of the land not only for survival and production, but also for pleasure and leisure, often associated with the advent of the first forms of art expression.[2]

Design, as I heard once from Nicholas Dines[3], is the use of art skills as a way to solve human problems and achieve aims. Landscape design is definitely the use of art to transform and shape natural systems into cultural systems, aiming beyond agro-production and encompassing other dimensions, namely recreation, aesthetic pleasure, art, and spirituality.

For centuries and even millennia of humankind's evolving cultural landscape, the assets of landscape design were mainly kept in and directed to the private realm. Their formal aesthetic patterns were predominantly inspired by the orthogonal and straight lines of agriculture, and enriched with irregular, curvy, and undulating lines probably inherited from pastoralism.[4]

With the Industrial Revolution of the 18th and 19th centuries, landscape desigers were called on to help in the search for solutions to the problems that arose witht he development of new cities. The visionary works of some landscape designers, such as Peter Lenée in Europe and Frederick Law Olmsted[5] in America, brought the know-how of garden art into the public domain, paving the way for the emergence of landscape architecture as a social art.

Thus the art of park and garden design for the public owe sits origin to, and is the consequence of, the evolutionary process that includes cultural landscape evolution in general and 18th-and 19th-century urban design in particular.

The first public parks already showed an awareness for the concern of land characteristics, namely the underlying functions of natural systems, hence the roots of ecological and sustainable design. The Park System of Boston—The Emerald Necklace—became a paradigmatic example of this attitude. The unhealthy wetlands that were constraining 19th-century Boston's urban expansion became an opportunity for city beautification and public amusement through the work of Olmsted.

All through the 20th century, ecology and the awareness of preserving a quality environment heavily influenced modern park design. Modern landscape aesthetics added the aim of conservation of nature and respect for the aptitudes of the land. Functionalism in modern landscape architecture became endowed with two dimensions: the public use, and respect for nature. If 19th-century parks owe a lot to English and German romantic landscape styles, modern parks were designed with the belief that the harmonious function of ecosystems would lead to beauty, and create adequate parks for intensive urban uses. Within this frame, optimizing maintenance routines and costs became a factor in modern park design.

Postmodern criticism claimed that park design should not only be aimed at public use, but include public participation as well. Bottom-up approaches to design were defended and included in many park and park-system designs in the second half of the 20th century, many of which became known as greenway design[6] , and extended their influence beyond their physical boundaries to larger areas through urban and landscape planning.

Also, postmodernism placed a focus on the cultural identity of artistic expression, which park design should definitely include in its methodologies. Garden and parks should not be restricted to their social and environmental functions. They should be places aiming to promote friendly atmospheres and ambiances, where people can experience a sense of belonging, and develop affections through what became known as topophilia.[7]

In addition, parks should be places to have fun, to surprise, to make people dream, and feel new experiences and sensations. Thematic parks, fairgrounds, allotments, botanical gardens, among other typologies, became noteworthy examples of contemporary park design. Concern for sustainable use of resources, and for the viability of large park systems in metropolitan areas, further stressed the significance of ecosystems, use of natural vegetation, and acceptance of each park by the community as unavoidable design drivers.

The origins of gardens and parks are related to cultural landscape changes, producing notably designed spaces that contrast with the surrounding natural landscapes. By way of contemporary park and garden design, nature—biodiversity resources and processes—is now participating in the invention of new places for people's enjoyment, happiness, and dreaming. This book intends to convey to the reader this rich diversity within the context of contemporary landscape design trends.

[1] Awarded with IFLA Sir Geoffrey Jellicoe Award 2014: Gonçalo Ribeiro. Telles, 1985. Para além da revolução. Lisboa. Editor Salamandra.
[2] Geoffrey Jellicoe and Susan Jellicoe, The Landscape of Man, Thames and Hudson, London, 1975.
[3] Professor of Landscape Architecture at University of Massachusetts, conversation in 2012 in 'The Fábos Conference on Landscape and Greenway Planning', University of Massachusetts, Amherst.
[4] A social and economic system based on the raising and herding of livestock, also supporting the concept of pastoralism as the quality or state of being pastoral, especially used in literature and painting.
[5] Frederick Law Olmsted, 'Public Parks and the Enlargement of Towns', in Richard Le Gates and Frederic Stout (eds), The City Reader: New York Routledge, 1996, pp. 337–44.
[6] Julius Fabos and Jack Ahern (eds), Greenways: The Beginning of an International Movement, Elsevier, Amsterdam, 1996.
[7] 'The Love for Places by Humans', in Yi Fu Tuan, Topophilia, Columbia University Press, New York, 1990.

Contents

Chapter 1 The Introduction of Country Parks

In the United Kingdom, the term 'country park' has a special meaning. There are around 250 recognizd country parks in England and Wales, attracting some 57 million visitors a year. Most country parks were designated in the 1970s, under the Countryside Act 1968, with the support of the former Countryside Commission. In more recent times, there has been no specific financial support for country parks, and fewer have been designated.

Most are managed by local authorities, although other organiztions and private individuals can also run them. There is nothing to stop anyone opening a site and calling it a country park, but they would not receive recognition or particular support from the government. Indeed, there are quite a few such private parks in existence, some of which are very far from what one might normally expect a country park to be.

The purpose of a country park is to provide a place that has a natural, rural atmosphere for visitors who do not necessarily want to venture further out into the wider countryside. Visitors can enjoy a public open space with an informal atmosphere, as opposed to a formal park as might be found in an urban area. For this reason, country parks are usually found close to or on the edge of built-up areas, and rarely in the wider countryside.

A country park usually has some formal facilities, such as a parking lot, toilets, maybe a coffee shop or kiosk, paths, and trails, and some information for visitors. Some have much more, with museums, visitor centers, educational facilities, historic buildings, farms, boating, fishing, and other attractions.

Many larger country parks organize entertainment for visitors, and are venues for fireworks displays, shows, and fairs, and other large, outdoor events.

There is not necessarily any public right of access to country parks, and visitors are usually subject to bylaws when they enter the park. Some charge for car parking; some are free.

These parks vary tremendously from one to another, and really have only their purpose in common: to provide easy access to the countryside for those living in the towns and suburbs. They often have an interest in nature conservation, although this is not necessarily the case.

Rogers Partners Architects+Urban Designers—Cody Canal Park

Chapter 2 The History and Development of Country Parks

Country parks were originally founded to protect sensitive areas of the countryside from the perceived threat of masses of urban, car-driving day-trippers. The concept of the country park, as a place to provide countryside-based recreational opportunities, clearly struck a chord. With substantial support being provided by the Countryside Commission, the initial slow start to the establishment and designation of country parks soon accelerated. Predominantly working in partnership with local authorities, the Countryside Commission successfully established, in two decades, around 250 country parks.

The support offered by the Commission was extensive: in addition to high levels of financial support to purchase land and establish park infrastructure, they also offered advice and guidance, and provided an officer contact point for every park. The support they offered was comprehensive and reached a level rarely seen since. The overall package of support was irresistible, and local authorities recognizd a good opportunity when they saw one. The rush to establish country parks was not strategically driven, and the criteria for designation was liberally interpreted, resulting in the creation of a broad range of country parks that were dispersed throughout the country. While the growth in country parks was rapid and not tightly controlled, many of the sites that were created were of high value. The majority of parks were located on the urban fringe, and many designed landscapes were included alongside other sites of great historic or environmental value. Strategically important areas of land, ideally positioned to limit urban sprawl, were also included. The large numbers of country parks that carry either important historic, environmental, or landscape planning designations verify the high strategic value of the land that was included in the great rush to establish country parks.

The Commission's remit was not one of perpetually supporting social initiatives; its job was to develop the concept, demonstrate what could be achieved, and influence local authorities and landowners to create and manage them. Despite this remit, the level of importance the Commission awarded country parks can be seen by their continued support for more than 25 years. Eventually the Commission's priorities began to move away from country parks to other social initiatives, and this is evidenced in the Commission's publications and internal reports. The reprioritization of the Commission's involvement coincided with sweeping reforms to local government and a period of reduced public spending. Consequently, at the point at which local authorities were expected to absorb an increasingly large share of the cost of providing country parks, their ability to do so was being continually undermined. A period of decline and under-investment, characterizd by stagnation and a lack of development, followed the Commission's withdrawal.

Strootman Landschapsarchitecten--Belvederes Drentsche Aa

Among the Countryside Agency's current priorities, the interface between urban and rural communities now features highly. The Agency has correctly identified country parks as a resource that can potentially contribute to improving that interface, thereby supporting rural economies and interpreting rural issues for an urban population. In addition, country parks have the capacity to contribute to social inclusion and diversity initiatives, another of the Agency's current priority areas of concern. The Agency must now determine how country parks can contribute to these important areas of work, what might prevent them from making an effective contribution, what resources are required to tackle and eliminate these barriers, and how these resources might be found.

2.1 The Original Country Parks Concept, 1966–1968

In the 1960s there was a widespread perception, among many politicians and policymakers, of an imminent crisis in the countryside. This was precipitated by several social factors, primarily the growth of leisure and recreation. In an influential article, Michael Dower wrote of what he called 'the fourth wave':

'Three great waves have broken across the face of Britain since 1800. First the sudden growth of dark industrial towns. Second, the thrusting movement along far flung railways. Third, the sprawl of car-based suburbs. Now we see under the guise of a modest word, the surge of the fourth wave which could be more powerful than all the others. The modest word is LEISURE.' The language is surprisingly pessimistic given that the growth in leisure was popularly viewed as one of the expected benefits of the widely embraced technological revolution of the 1960s. In 1971, a Countryside Commission report on country parks foresaw a threefold growth in countryside recreation over the next 30 years.

An increase in leisure time from one-and-a-half or two days per week to three or four days by the year 2000 was widely predicted. Both the Keele Pilot National Recreation Survey in 1967, and the Government Social Survey's (GSS) Planning for Leisure in 1969, saw a pattern of increasing population, increasing income, increasing mobility, and a rise in occupational class and educational status. This was the golden age of 'the pleasure drive,' the era of the Shell Book of Britain and the roadside picnic, with private cars becoming cheaper and the new road network expanding. The GSS survey recorded that 40 percent of those visiting Box Hill in Surrey had started off without the intention of making it their destination, while half the remainder (30 percent) were going on to another place, and 44 percent of visits to commons were incidental to the purpose of 'a drive into the country.'

This widespread belief in the imminence of a society of leisure went hand in hand with fear for the future of the countryside's special qualities. New leisure and mobility were viewed as a threat, as Dower had eloquently expressed. In 1974, the Countryside Commission's report, New Agricultural Landscapes, stated: 'While some recreational activities and wildlife conservation coexisted with little conflict until recently, the increasing intensity of both agriculture and recreation now threatens their coexistence on the same land.'

2.2 The Development of Country Parks, 1968–1992

The creation and designation of country parks immediately after the 1968 Act progressed slowly, but then between 1970 and 1972, it accelerated. This reflected not the founding of new parks, but the increasing qualification of existing sites for the country parks symbol. There was a second dip after 1977, then a leveling-off for the next 14 years, albeit with some slowing down after 1987. By 1991, there were 210 country parks established.

Before the 1974 Local Government Act, the Commission was required to restrict its spending to two specific programs—country parks/picnic sites, and long-distance routes—without any general powers to fund other projects. As a result, a number of good projects, which did not really fall into the required categories, were included as country parks (for example, the stretch of disused railway that became the Wirral Country Park). While praiseworthy in channelling funds into good projects, this may have had the effect of blurring the image of the country park.

2.3 Country Parks, 1992–1996

The early to mid-1990s saw the Commission increasingly interested in 'customer care' in the countryside. Following the 1989 review of Welcoming Visitors to Country Parks, the Commission published Visitors in the Countryside—Consultation Paper in 1991,which

Strootman Landschapsarchitecten--Belvederes Drentsche Aa

promoted means of improving visitor information, and their confidence, understanding, and care for the countryside.

Enjoying the Countryside: Policies for People (1992) undertook to 'develop a method to enable managers of major recreation sites to review the welcome offered to visitors in ways that lead to an improvement in the quality of the visitors' experience.' The text did not use the phrase 'country parks.' The promised methodology materialized in 1995 as the checklist published in the Visitor Welcome Initiative.

It was, however, purely voluntary in nature, and came with no associated grant package and no hidden agenda. It could be interpreted as the Commission's withdrawal not only from funding country parks, but also from seeing them as a distinct part of its own developing program. It should be stressed that this was not an unplanned withdrawal: the remit of the Countryside Commission was that of a 'research-station' for new initiatives, conceiving them, testing them, and then handing them on to enable it to continue pioneering. In some respects, country parks had a better run for their money than most programs, receiving significant spending for a considerable period.

Although a review of recreation sites had been proposed in the 1991/92 Corporate Plan, it did not occur. They remained a specific corporate program until dropped in the Corporate Plan for 1995/96, but this drift created 'a policy vacuum ... in relation to country parks and picnic sites in the contemporary countryside recreation context'; it also created the widespread misconception that the Commission had 'abandoned the resource as well as the concept' of the country park.

2.4 Country Parks, 1996–2005

Following the Select Committee report, the Countryside Agency commissioned research from the Urban Parks Forum (now Green Space) and the Garden History Society to investigate the potential for 'a renaissance in Country Parks.' It also set up a Country Parks Renaissance Advisory Panel (endearingly known as CPRAP), which later became the Country Parks Advisory Group. The research was presented in July 2003 in a report titled Towards a Country Parks Renaissance (Urban Parks Forum & Garden History Society, 2003). The Agency welcomed the report, referring to country parks as 'one of our forgotten treasures,' and acknowledging that 'country parks need more support if the contribution they make to recreation, the environment, the rural economy and the viability of villages, towns and cities is to be sustained or further improved.'

In May 2004, the Agency published its own conclusions in a Research Note Towards a Country Parks Renaissance (Countryside Agency, 2004). At the same time, the Agency offered funding to the Urban Parks Forum, which had set up a self-help network for country park staff in 2001. This has become the Country Parks Network (CPN), which has now established itself as a valuable tool for managers. Ninety percent of England's country parks are now in the Network; a bi-monthly newsletter is distributed, and regional events started in 2005. Two advisory panels, a strategy group and a delivery group, formed out of the original Advisory Group. They steer the Network and advise the Agency. In addition, the Agency has championed three pilot projects as part of the Renaissance research in 2002, tapping into the Heritage Lottery Fund, to demonstrate standards for country park management. Standards are the subject of further pilot projects currently being developed with the CPN. The Agency has also set up its own country parks website.

Rehwaldt Landscape Architects—Elbe Waterfront Park Riesa

Rehwaldt Landscape Architects—Elbe Waterfront Park Riesa

Chapter 3 Characteristics of Country Parks

3.1 Physical Characteristics

Using the questionnaire data, a country parks database was created that includes the name and address of the park, ordnance survey grid reference, size, and contact details. Each responding officer was also asked to provide a 50-word description of the park and detailed information about:

• Primary land type—predominant land type, such as woodland, grassland, or heathland.

• Use prior to designation—what the land was used for before it was designated or operated as a country park.

• Location—such as rural or urban fringe.

• Other land type—other types of land included within the boundary of the park.

• Historic park status—any official historic park designations, such as inclusion in the English Heritage Register of Parks and Gardens of Special Historic Interest.

• Nature conservation designations—any specific nature conservation designations, such as Local Nature Reserve or Site of Special Scientific Interest.

• Landscape planning designations—any specific planning designation awarded, such as Area of Outstanding Natural Beauty or Green Belt.

From the information provided, it was possible to record the details of the individual sites on the database—providing baseline data that could be used in any future audit process—and to examine the predominant physical characteristics that prevail throughout the range of country parks.

3.2 Primary Land Type

This information was provided by 134 of the responding parks, and the results are shown in Figure 1. Woodland was the most predominant primary land type, closely followed by parkland, and then grassland. Between them, these three categories accounted for 74 percent of responding parks. Coastal areas, heathland, and chalk/downland appeared seldom, collectively accounting for only 10 percent of responding parks.

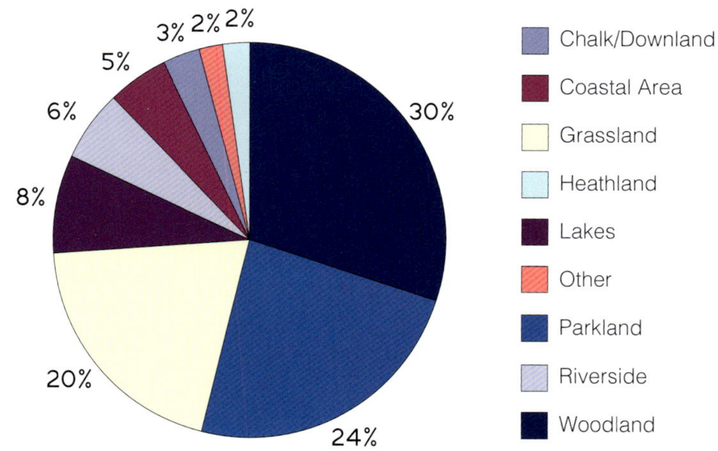

Figure 1 Breakdown of primary land type based on 134 responses

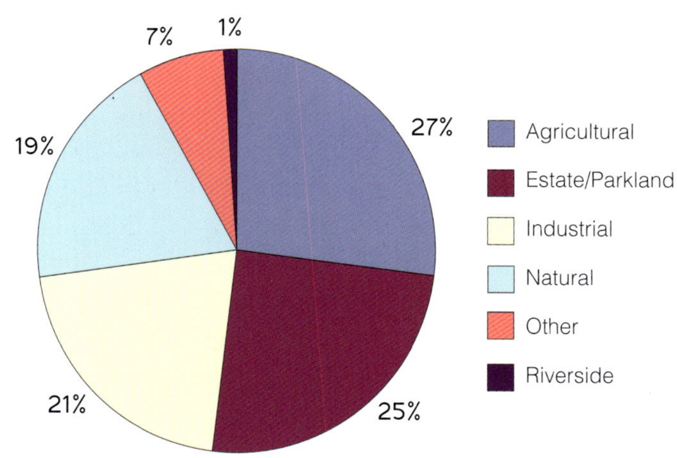

Figure 2 Prior use of country parks based on 137 responses

3.3 Prior Use

All of the respondents answered this question. The majority of country parks were formerly agricultural land, estate/parkland, or industrial sites, with scores of 27 percent, 25 percent, and 21 percent respectively. The data is illustrated in Figure 2, where 'Other' relates to three parks that listed their prior uses as public open space, disused railway line, and an army hospital site.

3.4 Location

The majority of country parks (65 percent), were found in urban fringe areas, 40 percent were found in rural areas, and just 1 percent was located in inner-city and industrial locations. However, some initial work by the Urban Parks Forum on the creation of a Geographical Information System (GIS) for country parks has taken place. This makes it clear that more than 65 percent of country parks are located within a few miles of a large town or city.

During the early stages of the creation of the GIS system, it was noted that there appeared to be a relationship between the geographic positions of country parks and the network of major roads and motorways. This suggests that the choice of where to create country parks was influenced more by the location and movement of urban populations than by the actual countryside that would surround the park.

3.5 Historic Status

Of the 137 parks that responded, 97 (71 percent) declared that they had no historic designations. Between them, the remaining 40 parks declared a total of 60 historic designations. Sites on the English Heritage Register of Parks and Gardens of Special Historic Interest were most frequent (15 percent), followed closely by sites of archaeological interest (13 percent) and scheduled ancient monuments (13 percent). The 'Other' consisted of sites of local interest or sites with historic remains. This data suggests that within the range of country parks, there was a historic and heritage value, with 29 percent of parks carrying at least one official historic designation. Figure 3 indicates which of the historic designations were most commonly found within country parks, and shows what percentage of parks carried each of the designations.

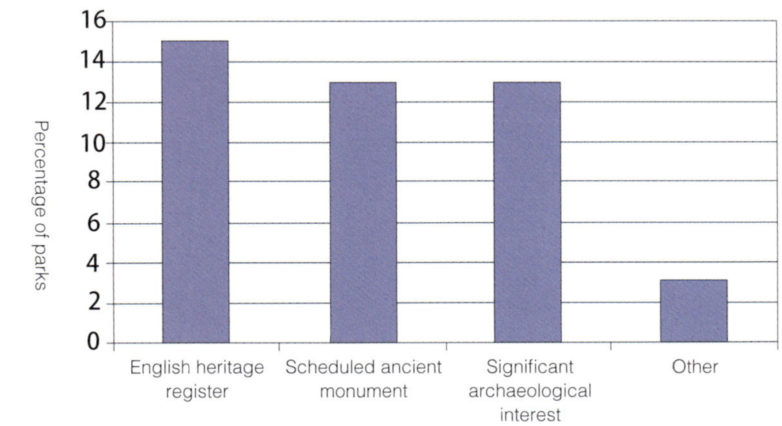

Figure 3 Historic designations based on 137 responses

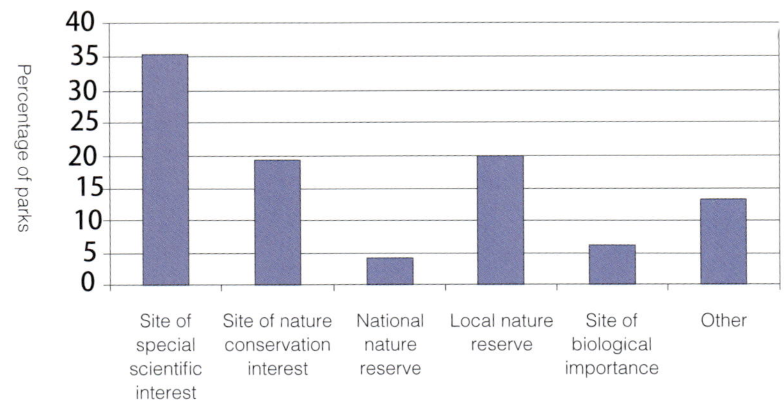

Figure 4 Nature conservation designations based on 132 individual designations from 88 parks

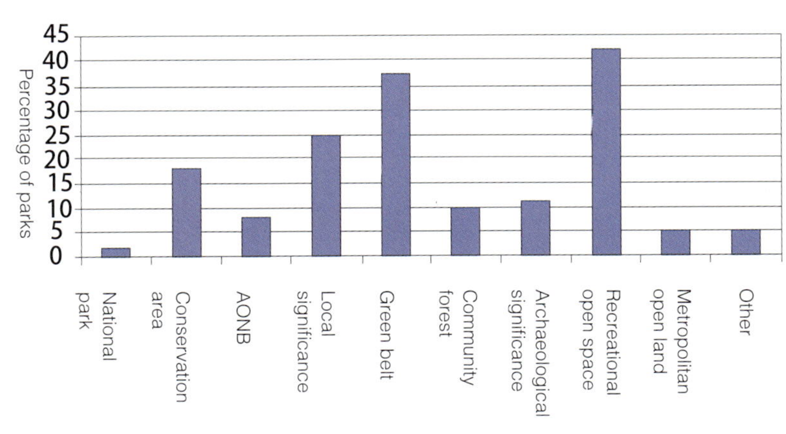

Figure 5 Landscape/planning designations based on 137 responses

3.6 Nature Conservation Status

Between them, 88 (64 percent) of the responding parks had 132 nature conservation designations, and 49 (36 percent) had none. The most common designation was that of Site of Special Scientific Interest (SSSI), representing 35 percent of all nature conservation designations applied to country parks. The two designations of Site of Nature Conservation Interest (SNCI) and Local Nature Reserve (LNR) were the next most common, representing 20 percent and 19 percent respectively of the nature conservation designations. These are illustrated in Figure 4. The large 'Other' bar in this chart comprises Ramsar sites (wetlands of international importance) and sites of local importance.

3.7 Landscape Planning Status

Landscape planning designations reflected the importance of these areas in planning terms. There were 225 landscape/planning designations within the 137 responding country parks. Figure 5 indicates which of the landscape planning designations were most commonly found within country parks, and shows what percentage of parks carried each of the designations. Recreational open space (42 percent), green belt (37 percent), and local significance (25 percent) were the most popular of landscape planning designations. The 'Other' comprised county wildlife sites, heritage coast, river valley, or great landscape value. Of the responding parks, 29 (21 percent) had no landscape planning designations.

Nádia Schilling, João Pombeiro--Projecto de Requalificação das Arribas

Nádia Schilling, João Pombeiro--Projecto de Requalificação das Arribas

Chapter 4 The Role of Country Parks

4.1 Recreation

The role of the country park was to provide a location for what the Countryside Recreation Research Advisory Group categorized as 'informal countryside recreation,' defined in 1970 as 'recreation, the main aim of which is relaxation which requires little in the way of special skill or organisation, which lacks any competitive element and which requires a countryside location for its full enjoyment.'

Zetter commented, 'The use of the word "informal" stresses the spontaneous, unsophisticated nature of the activities which typically include picnicking, playing informal games, walking short distances and driving for pleasure. This last activity is of great importance because not only does it rank as a major activity on its own, but it is usually an essential feature of a trip involving other activities as well.'

The Commission stated in its 1971 report The Evolution Of Country Parks Policy: 'the attributes of people who predominate in this type of recreation in England, speaking very generally, are that they reside in urban areas, are middle class, own cars and have young families.'

4.2 Protection of Vulnerable Land

The use of country park designation as a means of protecting high-quality landscapes, or strategic areas of open countryside, was not mentioned in early guidelines from the Commission. It was not until 1987 that their potential for 'safeguarding existing parkland' was recognized (Enjoying the Countryside: Priorities for Action).

However, in their liberal interpretation of the policy framework, the commissioners and field officers always had this consideration in view, and a substantial number of historic parks received grants as a result of country park designation.

As a result, it is noticeable that parks located in historic parkland, the bulk of which were laid out before 1987, rarely cover the complete designed landscape.

Many—Cannon Hall near Barnsley, Camer Park in Kent, Coombe Abbey near Coventry, Langley Park in Buckinghamshire, and Hardwick Hall in County Durham—extend to only a small part of the parkland. This has contributed to fragmented ownership and its concomitant problem of fragmented management.

4.3 Wildlife Conservation

Compared to modern levels of interest, the habitat value of country parks was initially little recognized. Countryside Commission Board papers from 1971–73, regarding country park grant applications, make little reference to wildlife conservation value or potential. A study in 1991 referred to important habitats being 'surprisingly well represented' in parks. Some parks, it went on, 'even contained or adjoined areas designated SSSI or local and national nature reserves.'

This omission has been well rectified by modern management planning, which tends, given the education and training of many country park managers, to be strong on nature conservation. A recent study concluded: 'The quality of habitat management was found to be extremely high and none of the parks visited fell below a satisfactory (Grade C) standard.'

At many sites there was tangible evidence of active management and enhancement works and considerable attention was often given to wildlife conservation interests. There were no instances in which recreational use of the parks appeared to seriously conflict with conservation interests, except in a few very localised cases.'

Fitzgerald Frisby Landscape Architecture,Andrew Lloyd—Toomuc Creek

Chapter 5 Design Criteria of Country Parks

The major difference between country parks and urban parks is in their geographic positions. Country parks, which are often located on the rural-urban fringe, are often crowded with visitors at weekends, which means the landscape should be designed based on tourist demand at the 'best time' rather than at peak times; in general, the former is about two-thirds of the latter.

5.1 Effective Land Area

Country parks can protect the ecological environment only if they cover a certain area of land, which plays a significant role in determining the diversity of species, habitat structures, and isolation status. In Britain, country parks should at least cover 10 hectares (24.7 acres); in Hong Kong, the smallest country park—Mount Longhu Country Park—covers an area of 47 hectares (116 acres), and the largest one—South Lantau Island Country Park—covers an area of 5640 hectares (13,937 acres), which effectively protects local natural resources together with North Lantau Island, and covers a total area of nearly 8000 hectares (19,786 acres).

5.2 Unique and Attractive Natural Landscapes

One of the main ways for country parks to attract more visitors is by holding various activities, including thematic activities, public meetings, wedding ceremonies, and family parties. For example, Oakwell Hall Country Park in West Yorkshire hosts an 'Apple Day' every year, encouraging more local children to visit the park.

This activity, with the theme of a good harvest, presents the whole production process from a single apple to a whole orchard; young students can discuss the apple harvest through painting, or writing a few words, expressing their respect for agriculture. Through such activities, local children can embrace the passion of country parks and feel encouraged to visit the park again.

Country parks can also be used as an open space for holding outdoor adventure activities. For example, the park administration department of Buchan Country Park in West Sussex—a place that used to be for timber production and land grazing but gradually evolved into wilderness—rebuilt the road network within the park, turning half of the paths into comfortable walking trails. As a result, the 2.2-mile (3.5-kilometer) race path across the wilderness has become an important signifier of the park and attracts a lot of local residents.

Table 1 Criteria for Country Parks in Britain

Primary criteria
At least 25 acres (10 hectares) area with a clear boundary
Convenience
Target populations have easy and free access
The park has environmentally-friendly transport policies or programs
Provides indoor and outdoor barrier-free facilities for the disabled and complies with barrier-free design standards, according to regulations
Offers additional facilities for the disabled, such as disabled access, special chairs, and outdoor benches; clear and intelligible information; and recreational facilities
Features
The park should be dominated by natural or semi-natural landscapes, such as forests, grasslands, wetlands, wilderness, and countryside
Part of the environment (natural or building) is worthy of preservation and value enhancement
Buildings cover less than 5 percent of the total area
Part of the environment (artificial or natural) has historic features, with value enhancement
Facilities
Paths and bikeways for easy access to various destinations; guideboards or site instructions
Outdoor recreational facilities, such as water-sports and extreme-sports facilities
Washrooms on-site or nearby
Health path/ service center/ restaurants/ bikeway or bridleways/ decorative arts with guide posts
The relationship between local communities and surrounding communities
Provides opportunities for residents, who can take an active role in the park's management and development
Launches external activities, hires local residents; invites the residents and local schools to participate in or hold activities in the park
Receives visitors in multiple ways to meet various needs of local communities
Reduces the part belonging to the community to improve flexibility
The relationships of local communities with the distant suburbs
Transportation network connected with distant suburbs, and public and free area connected with other paths
Management
Daily attendance of employees
Permanent employees
Providing implementation or management work for communities
Updating management plan every day
Annual management plan
Activities
Providing plans for public activities or educational activities
Walking or activities plan
Plans for promoting healthy lifestyles and environmental awareness activities
Information and interaction
Clear entrance sign
Providing detailed information and interaction about the site or other issues
Providing activities information related to visitors
Providing signs in different languages

5.3 Streamlined Landscape Recreation Facilities

Natural and semi-natural growing landscapes, including forest lands, grasslands, wetlands, wilderness, and countryside, dominate the country park, within which the building areas should not cover more than 5 percent of the total area. One-third of the country parks in Britain were designed by non-professionals and opened to the public with very simple infrastructures. Another example, from the Netherlands, is Spaarnwoude Country Park, which was built in 1960, and covers an area of 6919 acres (2800 hectares). Less than 30 percent of its total area is developed; however, with complete functional facilities, it has become very popular among local residents.

5.4 Environmentally-friendly, Energy-saving, and Ecological Materials and Technologies

Based on the idea of ecology first, most of the buildings and facilities in country parks should use local, natural materials. For example, Dalby Forest Visitor Center, which is located in Germany, took a series of measures to limit damage to the surrounding countryside, including using local timbers or natural, renewable materials; adopting storable energy, recycling schemes, and renewable energy systems (wind turbines and solar panels); covering building surfaces with latches, weeds, and crushed branches; and flushing toilets with collected and stored rainwater. These buildings and facilities can be recycled after they are no longer in use, leaving the minimum traces on the natural environment.

5.5 Humanized Space Layout

It can be seen (in Table 2) that more than 50 percent of all country parks in Britain have strolling and jogging paths, functional areas for holding activities, and areas for cycling and fishing, most of which are built for individual use, without the need for extensive facilities and equipment. Barbecue, sports, music, horse riding, and other communal activities in nature settings are very popular in country parks, meeting the community's need for basic social experiences. Visitors' preferences for recreational activities determine the spatial layout of country parks:

- Different types of strolling paths and open spaces designed for the aged should have enough space and directional signs.

Table 2 Preferred Activities in Country Parks in Britain

Activity	Percentage %
Interpretative walk or talk	85
Special thematic activities	76
Hiking competitions	62
Cycling activities	61
Fishing activities	54

Table 3 Various Needs of Different Target Groups

Targeted Visitors	Facilities	Services
Elderly people	Short routes; parking and instructions; appropriate guideposts; pleasant landscape design	Minimum service standards; different kinds of activities; code action areas; free activities
Disabled people	Appropriate guideposts and instructions; accessible routes, toilets, and parking	Guides and tours for the park; special activities
People on low incomes	Public transport	Guides and tours for the park; discounts on activities and transportation
Children	Play area; snacks and beverages; paths; activities designed for infants and young children of different ages; children's activity center	Minimum standard instructions; child-specific activities
Pets	Isolated space; pet litter boxes	Public supervision

Table 4 Special Thematic Activities

Targeted activity	Facilities	Services
Commercial activities, group activities, programs and major events, such as concerts or festivals	Special required facilities; conference facilities; service staff	Staff to prepare and operate the facilities
Large sports events	Maintainedsport facilities; GPS; parking lots; restaurants; network of connecting paths; safety facilities	Staff to manage the facilities and be involved in the planning, management, and preparation of the site and user forums.
Individual hikers, informal sports events	Exclusive space; signposted paths; parking lots; restaurants; network of connecting paths; safety facilities	
Explorers	Parking lots; signposted paths	

• Thematic celebration spaces should have convenient access and beautiful scenery, be adaptable for different occasions, and be able to accommodate some temporary structures for a certain number of people.

• Retain the wilderness area where people can carry out some adventure activities.

• The areas for typical group activities—picnics and barbeques—may not have fixed tables and seats, but may use natural and movable materials or encourage visitors to bring their own picnic rugs, which allows visitors greater freedom of movement, and the area a greater amount of flexibility.

5.6 Safety Protection Systems

Safety is always the focus of attention at rural–urban fringes, and must be reflected in every corner of country parks, such as appropriate visibility, good maintenance and supervision, permeability and freedom of roads, safe access, and the safety of women and children. Reasonable landscape design can effectively reduce crime and potential threats to the visitors who tend to select the areas with good permeability and feel a sense of safety there. When a bike path crosses a road, reasonably arranged protection and speed-reducing railings can allow cyclists to change their direction or reduce speed in advance. Road signs should clearly indicate the shortest route to the service center, so that in case of emergencies, people can return to the service center and get some help quickly. However, freedom and adventure are indispensable features of a country park, which should not prevent visitors from freely experiencing the environment by imposing strict regulations. Crowded spaces should have a broad view, reducing the potential threats to visitors; roadside shrubs need to be trimmed in a timely manner, reaching a balance between ecological protection and personal safety.

Signs should inform visitors about potential risks, including the types and degrees of the risks as well as any preventive measures they can take. Responsibility is shared between visitors and park management, which must reasonably estimate what responsibility visitors can bear, to what extent the visitors will not harm other visitors, and how effectively parents, guardians and organizers can take charge of their children and tourists in the environment. Park management should make a risk analysis of the park, and develop a safety scheme, in which the risk control measures should be continuously updated. Visitor safety schemes must be continuously monitored and developed through the observation and analysis of visitors' behaviors, so as to keep visitors away from potential risks.

5.7 Detailed Management Measures

Country parks have a variety of facilities that are suitable for visitors with different needs, making the parks an ideal place for urban residents to enjoy beautiful landscape, ecological environment, and biological diversity (Table 3). Country parks are also ideal places for holding various group and individual activities, which extends the service range of country parks, expands their popularity, and allows more visitors to experiencewilderness activities that are different from those held in the cities (Table 4).

Fitzgerald Frisby Landscape Architecture, Andrew Lloyd—Toomuc Creek

Chapter 6 The Future of Country Parks

6.1 A Sustainable Future for Country Parks

To ensure an improved and more sustainable future for country parks, a process of change needs to be put in place. Achieving this aim requires a two-strand approach:

(1) Strategic Development

Strategic development of the country park service requires the following key elements:

- A commitment to prevent further undermining of the country park brand.

- Reinforcement of the country park image through enhancement and consistency of services and visitor experiences.

- The use of incentives to encourage the participation of all country parks in the process.

- The development of a vision for country parks that could be shared by all.

- The adoption of the gateway concept as a shared theme for all country parks.

- The development of a set of eight core areas of activity that all country parks would address to some degree, and relate this involvement to the visitor.

- The development of a set of minimum standards adopted by all.

- The establishment of a partnership-based strategic working group; this should comprise organizations that directly benefit from the ability of country parks to deliver their organization's policy objectives and that have access to resource opportunities.

(2) Delivery Methods

Delivery methods designed to create improvements require the following:

- Dissemination of information through the activities of the Country Park Network.

- Establishment of incentives, increased access to funding opportunities, awards that recognize excellence and improvement.

- Ensure that country parks are included in local authority parks and green-space strategies.

- Widespread use of a standardized self-audit database.

- Creation of a country park register and a guide to country parks.

- An increased emphasis on the delivery of services for 'people' rather than 'place'.

- Specific research into training needs and opportunities, management plans, management structures, customer surveys, and identification of good practice, and dissemination of the information.

- The establishment of a delivery or practitioner group to facilitate and inform the work of the strategic working group.

- Specific research into how the demand for new country parks is best met.

6.2 Country Parks Today

This review of country parks reveals a picture that is not altogether unsurprising, and follows on from the findings in the Public Parks Assessment 1. Four out of five parks using the name 'country parks' have been through the designation process. Nearly 65 percent of parks lie within the urban fringe, and many more lie on the main national road networks within easy access of large conurbations. Most parks are either sites of historic and/or conservation interest, and nearly 80 percent have at least one landscape planning designation.

However, many parks are reported as improving (54 percent), and this probably reflects the strong focus of many of these parks on nature conservation, which will improve over time. While it is estimated that total expenditure on country parks is in the region of £62 million, data shows this would need to be increased by around 28 percent to take spend to the level of the early 1980s. The same conclusions can be drawn for country parks as for their urban counterparts: good parks are getting better and poor parks are getting worse.

Country parks are clearly important to many people. Around 2500 people are employed in managing and maintaining country parks, and 98.5 percent of all country parks have, on average, three or more volunteer groups associated with them. An impressive 73 million visits are made to country parks each year.

6.3 Relevance of Country Parks to Our Future

When country parks were first conceived and established, their primary aim was to provide countryside-based recreational opportunities. Alongside this aim, they also successfully acted as mechanisms for protecting vulnerable land, and as wildlife conservation centers. Just like their urban counterparts, country parks are now expected to demonstrate that they can play a role in delivering services across a much broader social agenda. Country parks and the activities they provide should therefore address social inclusion, sustainability, community engagement, education, health, crime, social economies and heritage. Their ability to contribute to 'the bigger picture' will largely determine how much support and commitment they receive, both from the government and from grant organizations.

Country parks can become more successful if they can be shown to address many of the national issues facing government today. For example, country parks can contribute to policy aims on:

• Health—via participation in sport and recreation, including walking and green gyms, and through the ability of green space to relieve stress-related symptoms.

• Social inclusion—by providing access for the elderly, the disabled, and other groups, and as places where a wide cross-section of society can communally enjoy a quality environment.

• Culture, sport, and the arts—as venues in their own right, as quality environments, and for a diverse range of events.

• Employment—through education, training, and lifelong learning programs for staff and students, as well as active members of community groups.

• The needs of children and young people—by providing safe and stimulating environments for play, learning, social interaction, sport, and recreation.

• Sustainability—by acting as examples of good practice, utilizing sustainable resources and operational methods.

• Biodiversity—through their contribution to local and national biodiversity action plans, and the active conservation and enhancement of nature and wildlife within the park and surrounding areas.

• Community engagement and active citizenship—by engaging the local community and park users, by supporting community-based groups, and by offering opportunities for participation and volunteering in a wide range of activities, including manual tasks, visitor welcoming, and management.

• Linking town and countryside—many country parks link town and country physically because of their urban fringe location. Research for the Countryside Agency by the University of Manchester—on sustainable development of the countryside around towns—has identified the urban fringe as a landscape in transition. Its role as an important bridge to the wider countryside is complemented by its ability to provide land for 'a combination of agricultural production, physical space, and settings for residential use and recreation.' The research covers not only development pressure and the difficulties facing farmers, but also the relevance of green spaces to the quality of life in urban areas. It concludes that the urban fringe is 'the main area and a "learning zone" for sustainable development.'

Country parks serve important functions on the urban fringe, both in conserving strategically important green space, and in providing recreational opportunities for both rural and urban dwellers.

• Tackling the urban/rural divide—country parks link town and country socially and culturally. Their principal users comprise urban or suburban dwellers making visits to the countryside. 'For the majority of the population, the urban fringe is their first experience of the countryside.'

• Heritage and tourism—country parks have the potential to play an important role in local tourism, especially where they are based in a heritage property such as Rufford Country Park in Nottinghamshire, or Sir George Staunton Country Park in Hampshire. Normanby Hall Country Park, in Scunthorpe has been reinvigorated by a Heritage Lottery Fund award to restore its Victorian kitchen garden, and is now attracting tourists drawn by that particular feature. This aspect of country parks is often under-estimated by managers and local authorities.

• Education—country parks can provide important educational opportunities, not only in terms of the national curriculum but also in terms of allowing a general appreciation and understanding of the countryside and countryside matters.

Observations made during this review would suggest that there are numerous examples of country parks contributing to these and many more social issues.

For example, in one country park there was evidence of drug abuse on the site, and the problem appeared to be increasing. Working in partnership with the local police and specialist outreach workers, the rangers received training to enable them to identify the different types of substance abuse, make contact with the drug abusers, and direct them towards professional help. As a consequence, drug abuse on the site was reduced, and syringes and other drug paraphernalia were fewer and were removed more efficiently.

At Oakwell Hall Country Park, park staff actively sought to tackle racism and encourage more of the substantial local Asian community to visit the site. To achieve this, they made use of 'Apple Day', discussed earlier.

The park targeted local schools, inviting one school with a high percentage of Asian pupils and one with high percentages of white pupils to work together on the event. The pupils were asked to develop jointly a presentation to their own families and park visitors on the theme of 'Harvest'. To ensure that the pupils' families were present, the park arranged free transportation for both school groups.

The event was hugely successful, resulting in excellent interaction between the pupils, and encouraging them to celebrate not only the harvest, but also the cultural diversity of their local community. As a consequence of this initiative, there are now higher numbers of Asian families regularly visiting the park.

There is an urgent need to identify and examine these good-practice examples, produce guidelines that will allow the critical elements of each to be understood and replicated by others, and disseminate the information throughout the range of country parks.

Rogers Partners Architects+Urban Designers—Cody Canal Park

* Please note, the information provided in these introductory guidelines is specific to the United Kingdom, however, much of the background detail is for reference, and some of the general principles outlined here may be relevant to landscape architects and landscape designers of country parks across the globe.

References:

Natural England: *Towards A Country Parks Renaissance*

1. Countryside Commission, *Enjoying the Countryside: Policies for People* (CCP 371) 1992

2. Countryside Commission, *The Visitor Welcome Initiative*, (CCP 476) 1995

3. ibid. p.1, ibid. p.40, ibid. para.2.8

4. In E W M Holdaway, *The Country Park: an examination of its principles*, MSc unpublished thesis, University of Edinburgh, 1971, p.34

5. *J A Zetter, The Evolution of Country Parks Policy*, CCP 48, 1971, p.4

6. Michael Dower, *The Fourth Wave*, London: Civic Trust, 1966

7. Public Parks Assessment (May 2001): A survey of local authority owned parks, focusing on parks of historic interest, undertaken by the Urban Parks Forum

8. Quoted in Cara Aitchison, Nicola MacLeod, Stephen Shaw, *Leisure and Tourism Landscapes: Social and cultural geographies* (Routledge, London, 2000), p.64

9. Ray Woolmore, *111 parks in six years*, Geographical Magazine, July 1974, vol.66, no.10, pp.550-55

10. This assertion is based on reading a sample of fifteen Commission Board Papers on *Country Park grant applications 1971-73*

11. University of Manchester for the Countryside Agency, *Sustainable development of the countryside around towns, 2002*

Zhu Xiang-ming and Sun Qin, *'Character and Design Principles of Country Parks in the UK', Chinese Landscape Architecture, Issue 6, 2009, pp. 1–5*

Percorso Paesaggistico Culturale

Location: Borgo Virgilio, Italy
Area: 400 square meters (4305 square feet)
Landscape Design: Archiplanstudio
Photography: Martina Mambrin
Client: Amministrazione Borgovirgilio + Parco Mincio

The Percorso Paesaggistico Culturale park forms part of the Mincio Regional Park, and is defined by a series of lightweight structures that encourage visitors to interpret the history and culture of the local environment.

A series of installations were constructed and placed throughout the park, which have as their main cultural attraction the figure of the Roman poet Virgil and the integration of his poetry with the contemporary Mincio River landscape. The installations are configured as rest areas, which mark and measure the pedestrian path that runs along the bank of the river.

Examples of these installations include a 'courier door,' which represents an ancient post road, with its vertical structure emphasizing its geographical position. The 'gate of the fort' identifies a crossroads and marks the presence of a nearby fort in Pietole, from which it takes the figures of the ramparts. The 'Bucoliche door' is a metaphorical frame on a landscape fragment described in Virgil's *Eclogues*. The structure is set deliberately low to reduce its visual impact and fit the undulations of the landscape. The 'door of the Georgics' is located in front at an ancient court, and the architecture is intended to celebrate the balance between nature and man's work as sung by Virgil. The 'door of Travata' is located where a pumping station once

existed in the early 20th century, and celebrates man's attempt to govern the natural element of water.

These installations, and the park as a whole, offer a historical, cultural, and environmental interpretation of the area.

Top: The door overlooking the agricultural landscape
Bottom: Detail of the bike rack and seat

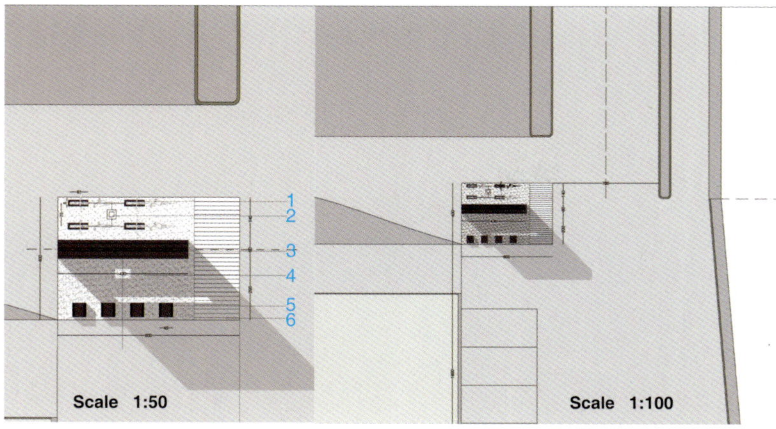

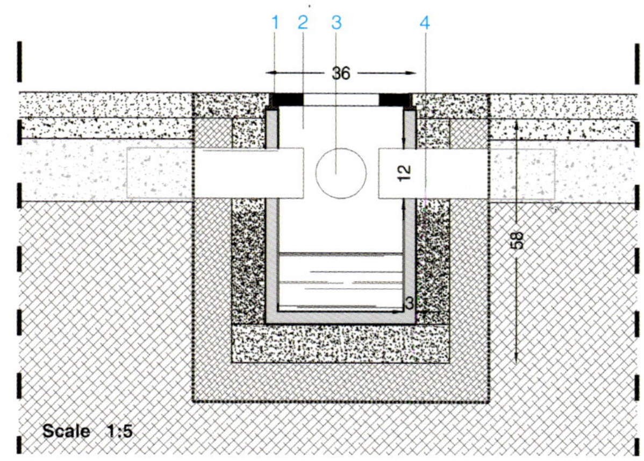

General Plan

1. Bicycle iron rack
2. Sump rainwater resulting from bicycle rack
3. Wall with steel and wood trim, black with window jambs in sheet steel, and inclined support for didactic panel
4. Paving cobblestones with underlying layer of reinforced concret
5. Seat made from shaped profile in galvanized steel
6. Reinforced concrete pavement and paving slabs made from sandblasted steel

Particular Sump Rainwater Resulting from Bicycle Rack

1. Plate door floor
2. Cockpit concrete internal
3. PVC pipe
4. Abutment of the well with concrete casting

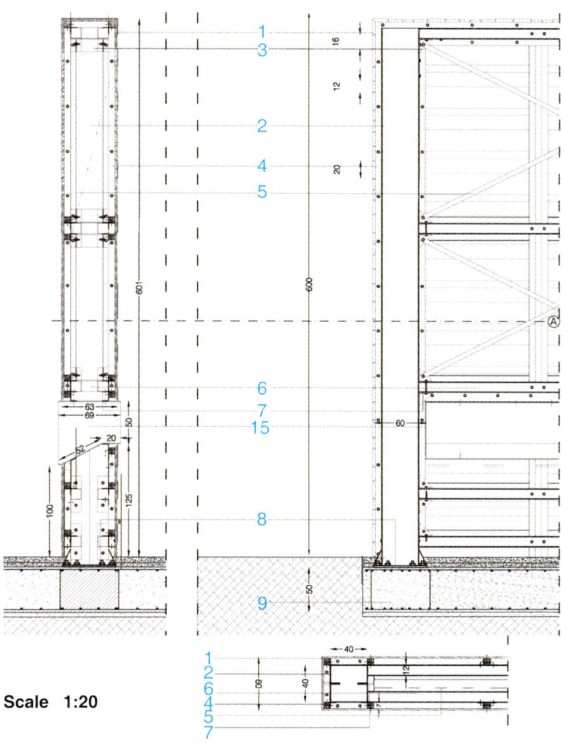

Scale 1:20

Longitudinal Section and Cross Portal Covered with Wood

1. Coating wooden slates
2. Pillars
3. Angular profile
4. Wooden laths on which to apply the coating
5. Plate
6. Profiles square bracing of the portal
7. Angular profile for fixing the horizontal bracings
8. Base plate anchored to the foundation using screws and chemical concrete
9. Foundation in reinforced mesh
10. Steel profile, smooth bike rack recessed
11. Duct drainage polymer
12. PVC drain pipe
13. Package consists of paving layer of thick concrete and entrapment
14. Seat made from steel foot
15. Steel structure in sections and coating steel sheet

Scale 1:50

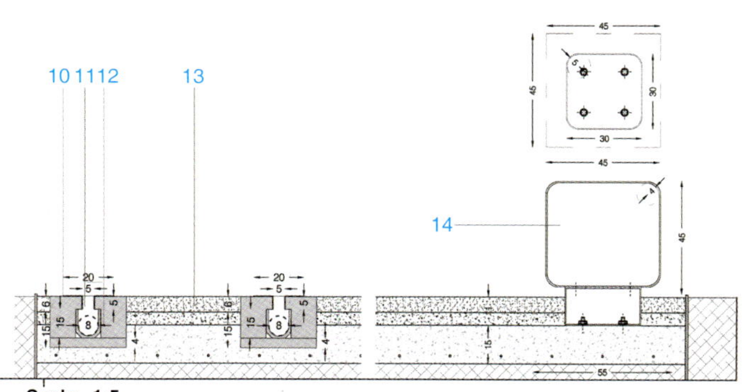

Scale 1:5

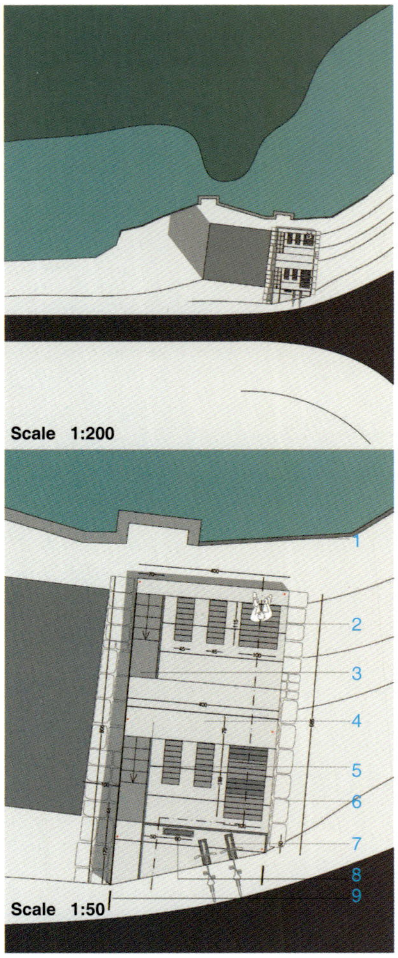

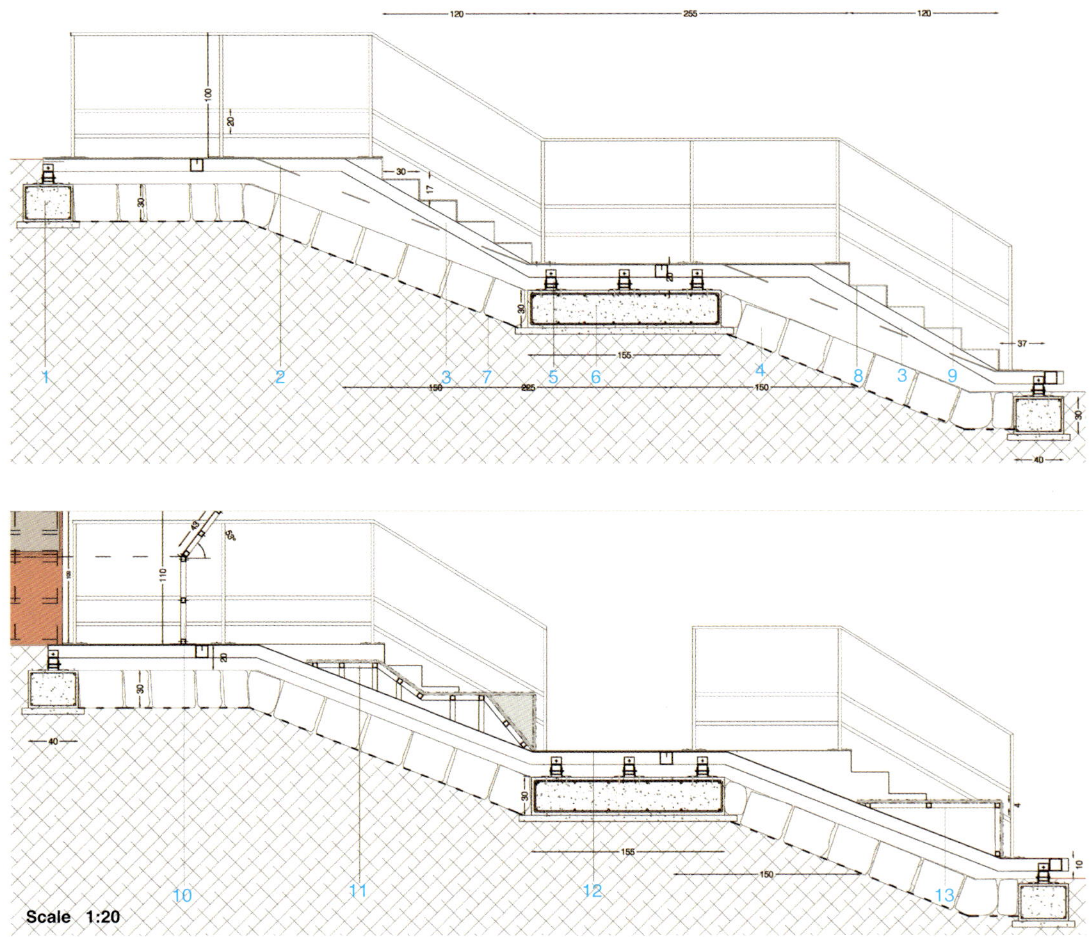

General Plan

1. Parapet to be painted
2. Seat covered in wood painted black
3. Scale diamond plate bent on structure profiles paintings
4. Paving slabs in iron rustication
5. Parapet formed by vertical and horizontal paltes and handrail section
6. Roadbed bank protection
7. Bicycle rack slits
8. Totem
9. Bow bollards

Detail of Staircase

1. Reinforced concrete foundation beam and brackets
2. Structure in paintings
3. Profiles square cross bracing
4. Roadbed bank protection made in boulders with the underlying layer geotextile grouted sand and cement
5. Adjustable feet for leveling of the structure and the respective anchor to the foundation
6. Reinforced concrete foundation beam and brackets
7. Geotextile
8. Staircase with steps in bent sheet metal embossed in square profiles
9. Iron railing with handrail, square pillars, and crossbars
10. Totem sheet supporting structure profiles, didactic panel with digital printing
11. Chaise lounge painted black with underlying structure in square profiles
12. Footboard covered in steel
13. Seat covered in painted wood with underlying structure in square profiles

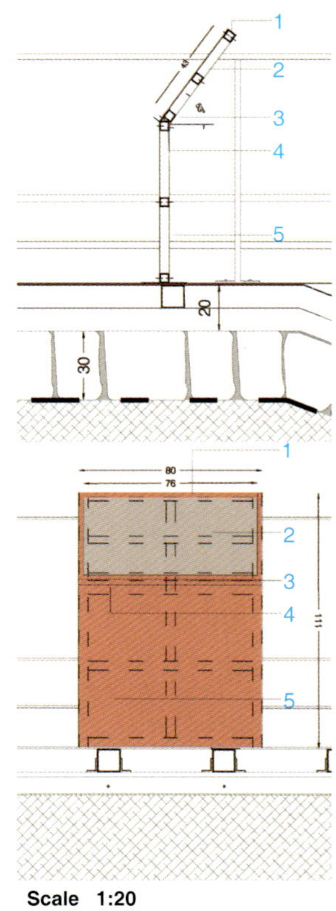

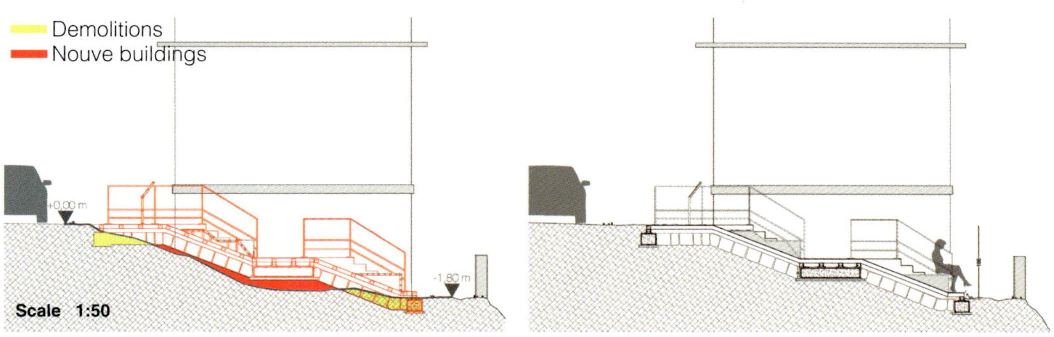

Totem Particular

1. Profiled rusty steel
2. Didactic panel with digital printing
3. Sturcture profiles square section
4. Angular junction
5. Metal caldding

Top: The Travata, located next to reclaimed buildings
Bottom left: Detail of the seats
Bottom right: Detail of the stairs

Top and bottom: The door of the fort is on several levels and works to frame a fragment of the landscape

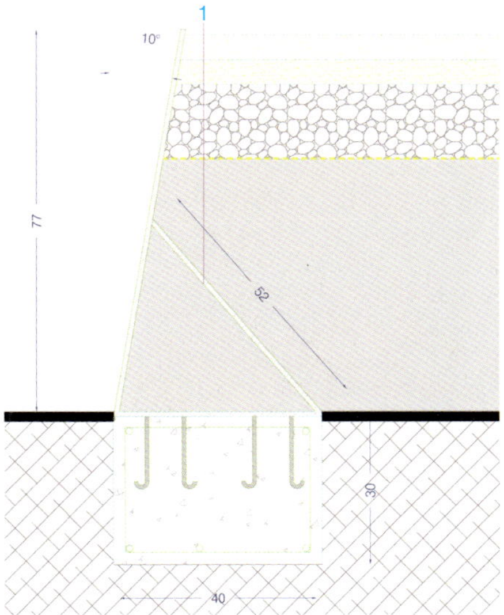

Particular Embankment Steel Blades

1. Blades made of sheet steel bent for anchoring to the foundation through bolts

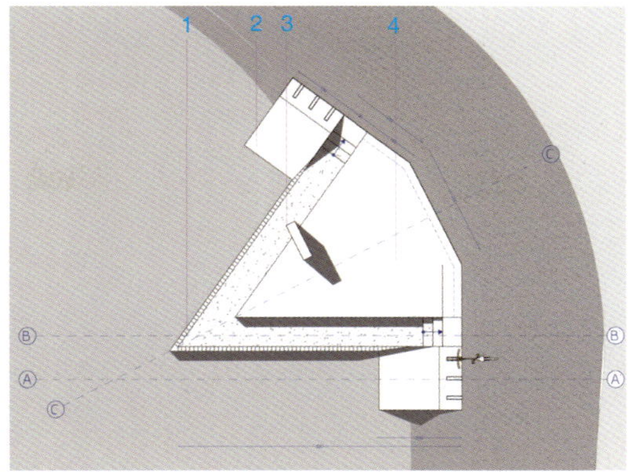

General Plan

1. Blades made of sheet steel bent for anchoring to the foundation through bolts
2. Slab formwork in reinforced concrete with surface oxides
3. Totem sheet steel mounted on rails
4. Foundation/bench in propeller with oxide red

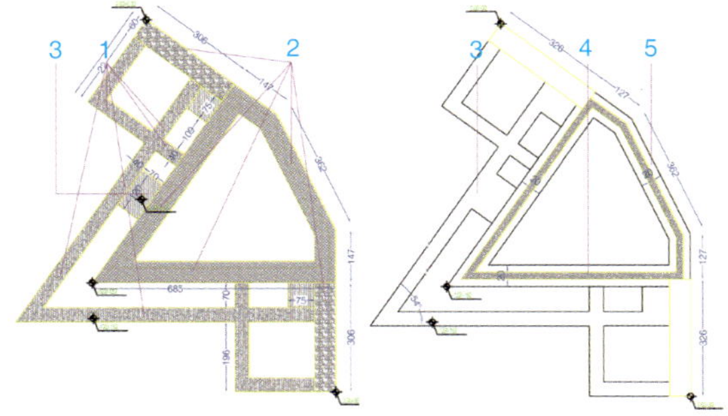

Scheme Foundation and Walls

1. Foundation
2. Foundation
3. Concrete slab share lowerec for totem
4. Load-bearing walls of the foundation
5. Enlargement curb to share bank

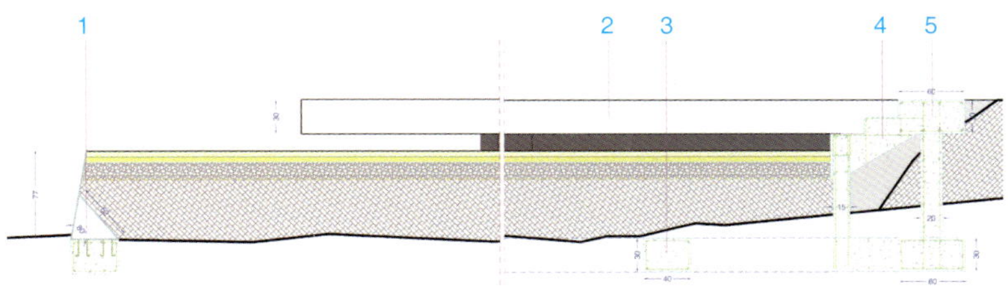

Section B-B

1. Blades made of sheet steel for anchoring to the foundation through bolts
2. Foundation/bench
3. Foundation beam
4. Steps in slab carrier
5. Foundation

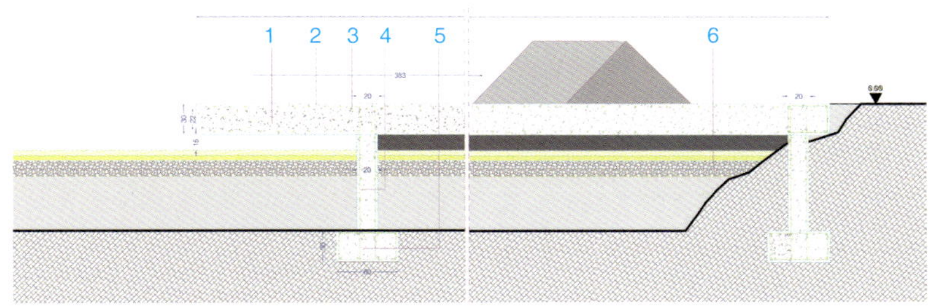

Section

1. Foundation/bench
2. 11 irons bent
3. 3 clips
4. Wall embankment
5. Foundation curb with brackets
6. Floor composed of soil and geotextile

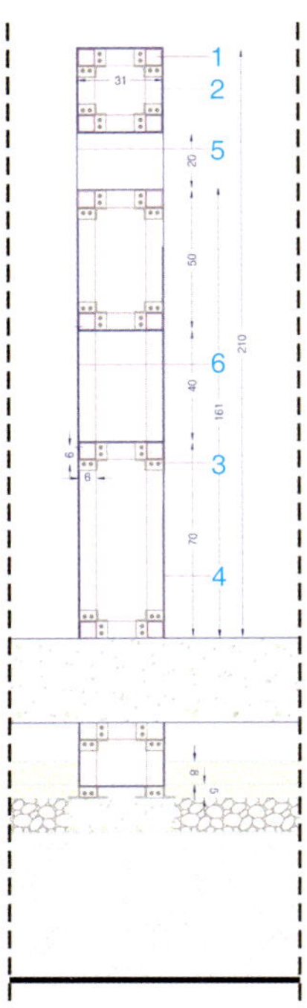

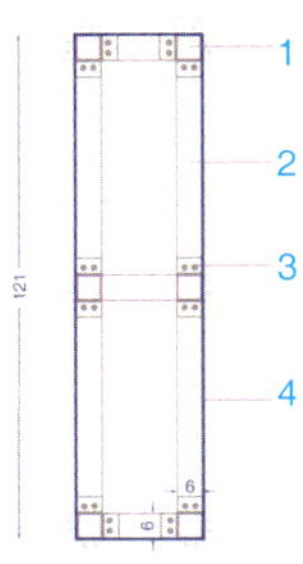

Totem Cross Section and Plant

1. Vertical square profiles
2. Horizontal square profiles
3. Angular anchor structure through special screws
4. Sheet of coating
5. Horizontal slot
6. Didactic panel screwed to the profiles

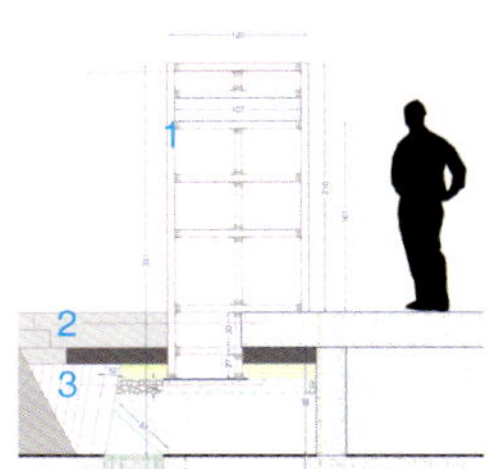

Totem Particular Node-slab

1. Structure of the totem in square profiles fixed to the concrete slab
2. Concrete foundation
3. Base in reinfirced concrete with mesh

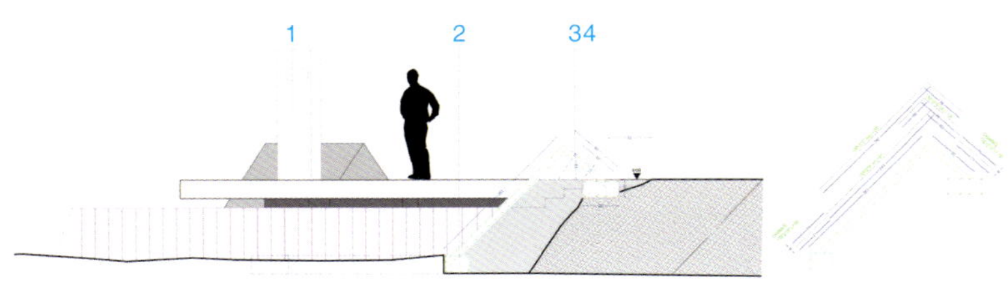

Section A-A

1. Totem rusty sheet steel mounted on structural steel section
2. Foundation curb section
3. Slab thrown against the ground reinforced with iron; the location of the bike rack level embankment is made by the pre-positioning of polystyrene templates to measure
4. Bicycle rack

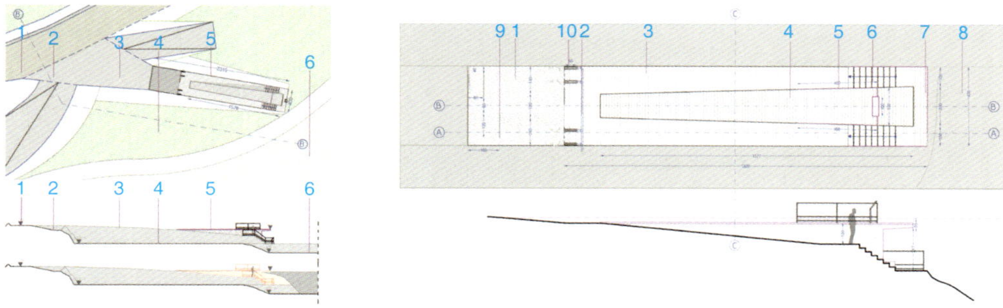

Plan and Section A-A

1. Ground
2. Door bike made with steel profile sunk in the ground with underlying drainage duct
3. Paved ramps with iron sandblasted planks, with welded bolts on the lower face
4. Coating bench in wood plank
5. Iron railing composed of flat vertical and horizontal
6. Steps paved with iron plates, sandblasted consistent with the rest of the pavement
7. Totem made of square profiles with inclines to support the educational panel with digital printing
8. Preseeded towels to be prepared on all embankments side to the ramps
9. Bow bollards reclining color
10. Rainwater collection system arising from the bike rack made through conduit PVC

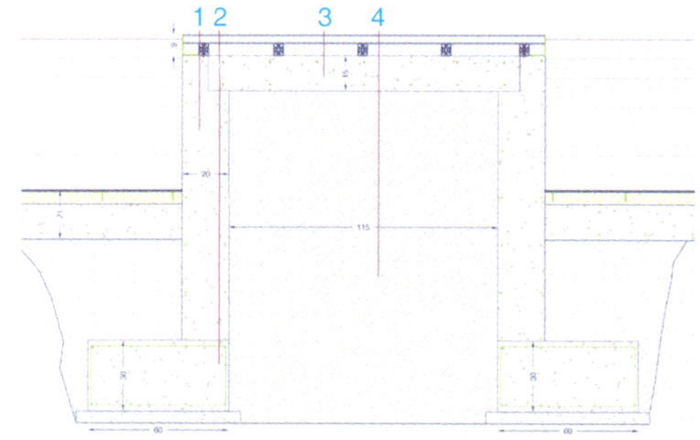

Section C-C

1. Muro strutturale in cls a vista conossidi rossi sp.20cm armato con 1+1 rete elettrosaldata diam.8mm dim.20×20cm
2. Fondazione sez.60×30cm armata con 4+4 diam.12mm e staffe diam.8mm passo 25cm L 184 e chiamate 1+1 diam.8mm p.20cm L 100cm
3. Soletta in cls sp.15cm armata con 1+1 rete elettrosaldata diam.6mm dim.20×20cm
4. Terreno di riempimento

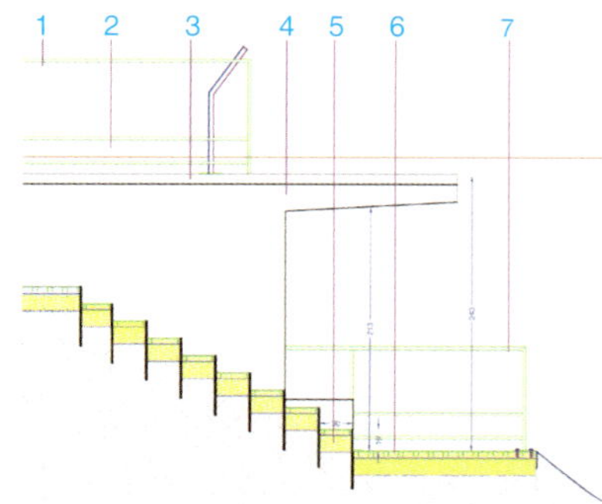

Particular of the Section A-A

1. Parapet steel plates anchored to the ground with base plates and screws sunk in chemical cement directly into the base and handrail
2. Dishes transoms para foot
3. L profile with outer coating in wooden planks with
4. Concrete structure with cantilevered slab
5. Steps made from steel, a layer of concrete, a bedding layer, and sandblasted iron plates
6. Floors made from 15cm of concrete reinforced with welded mesh Floors made from iron plates sandblasted with welded bolts on the lower surface
7. Totem made of square profiles

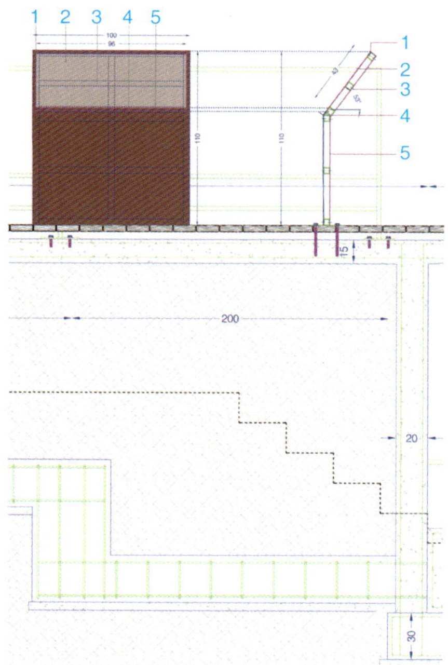

Prticular Section of the Totem

1. Profiled rusty steel
2. Didactic panel with applied digital printing
4. Angular junction
5. Rusty metal cladding

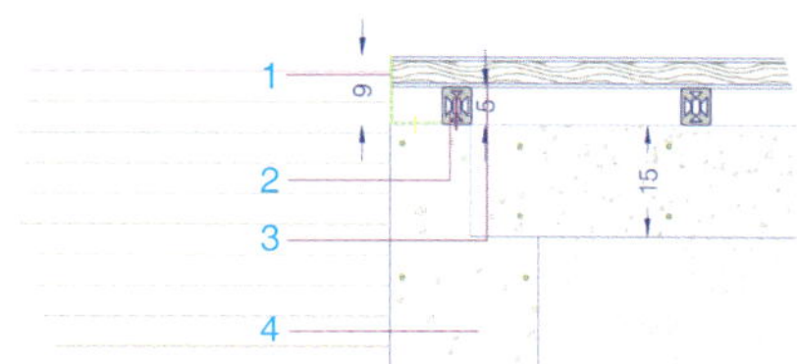

Special Coating Bench

1. L profile
2. Magatello in WPC
3. Coated wooden planks
4. Structural concrete wall with exposed oxide

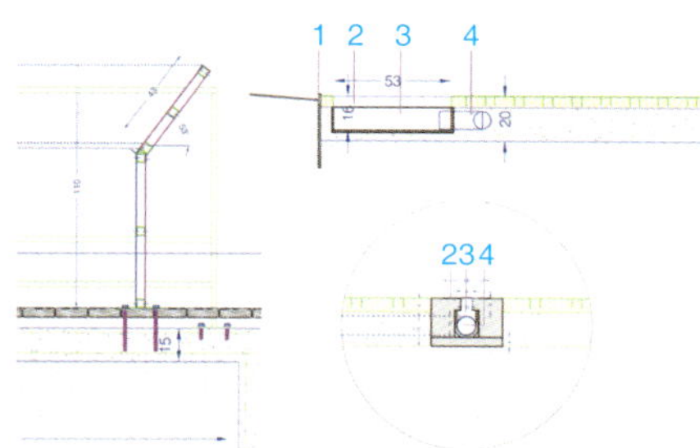

Particular Section of the Bycicle Rack

1. Curb steel
2. Profile in smooth steel
3. Duct drainage polymer
4. PVC drain pipe

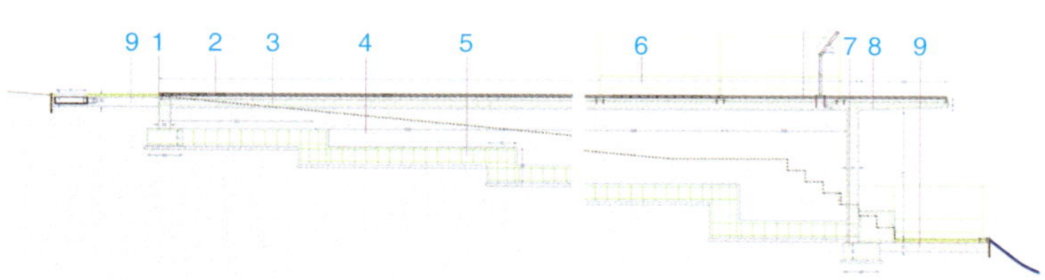

Section B-B

1. L profile
2. Coated wooden planks
3. Concrete slab reinforced with mesh
4. Backfill
5. Conci disdipi foundazione in cls
6. Iron railing
7. Foundation section reinforced with brackets
8. Cantilevered concrete reinforced with iron transverse diameter
9. Floors made from concrete reinforced with welded mesh

Top: The door of the Georgics stands out in the landscape
Bottom: The view on Corte Virgiliana

Side Elevation

1. Embankments
2. Bench with steel structure and seat covered in black painted wood
3. Laminated wood pillars painted black
4. Current ground profile

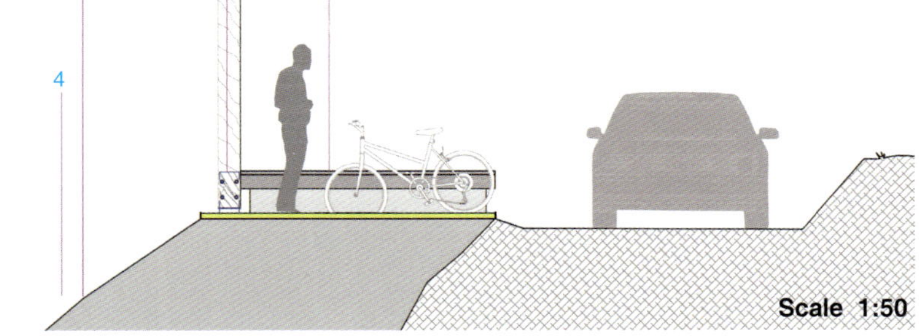

Scale 1:50

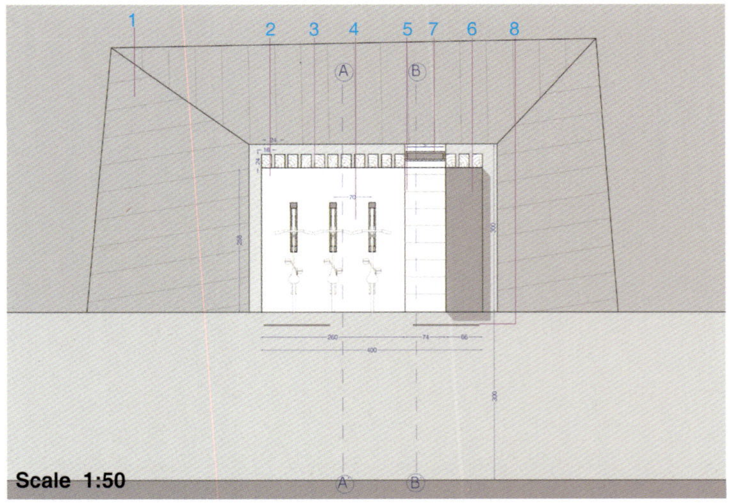

Scale 1:50

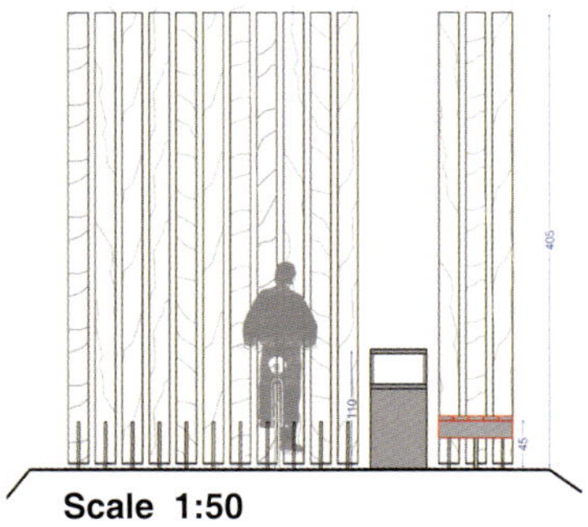

Scale 1:50

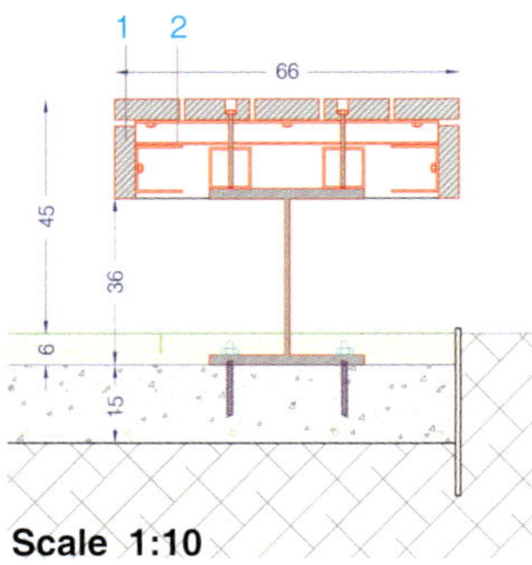

Scale 1:10

Bench Details

1. Structure in square profiles
2. Wood trim painted black

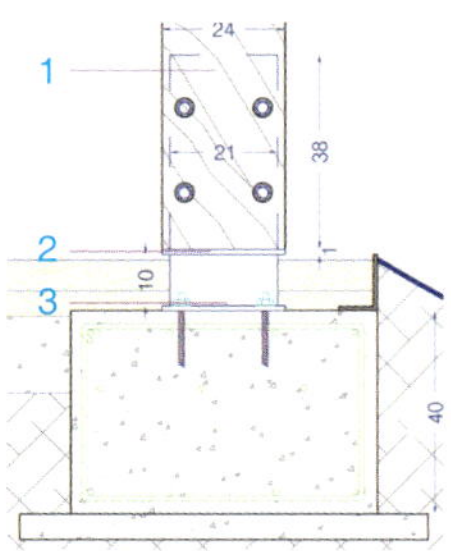

Scale 1:5

Node-pillar Foundation

1. Steel core inserted in the milled abutment created in the center line to the short side
2. Flat steel core welded
3. Flat base anchored to the foundation by means of blocks and chemical cement

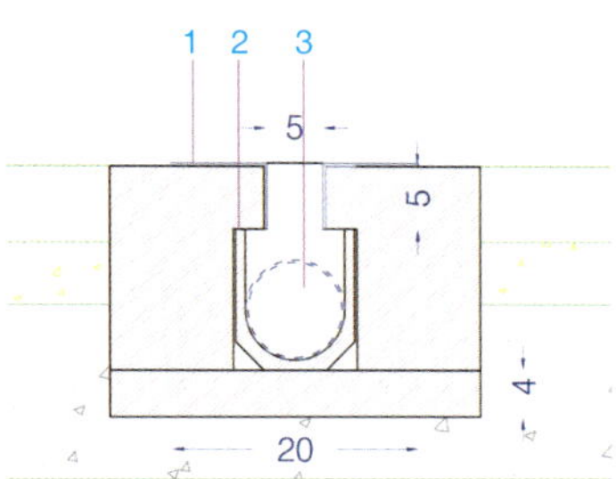

Scale 1:5

Bicycle Rack Details

1. Steel profile
2. Duct polymer drainage
3. PVC drain pipe

General Plan

1. Embankments
2. Paving cobblestones
3. Laminated wood pillars painted black
4. Bicycle rack steel recessed
5. Flooring iron sandblasted planks
6. Bench with steel structure and cover in wooden slats
7. Totem steel frame profiles square and rusty metal cladding
8. Bow bollards

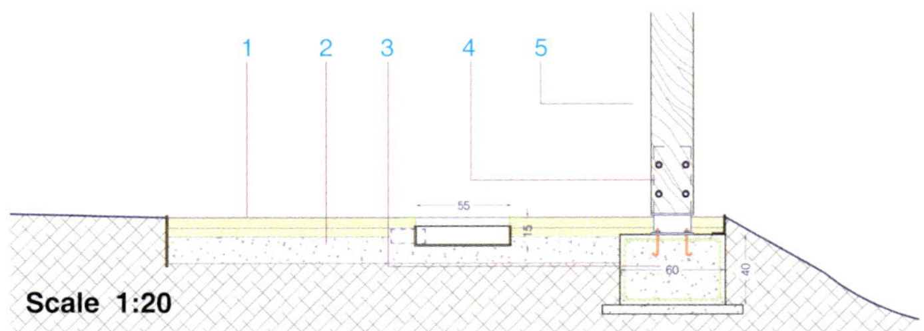

Scale 1:20

Section A-A

1. Paving cobblestones
2. Slab flooring
3. Foundation curb
4. Flat steel to support the wooden pillar
5. Wooden pillar painted black

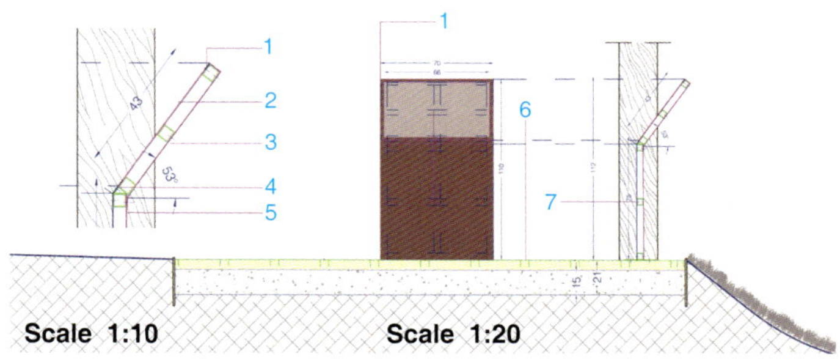

Scale 1:10 Scale 1:20

Section B-B

1. Profiled rusty steel
2. Wooden panel with applied marine digital printing screwed to the structural profiles
3. Structure profiles square section
4. Angular junction
5. Rusty metal cladding
6. Coating of flooring planks sanded on a bedding layer and underlying layer of reinforced concrete
7. Totem in profiled square

Top: The profile of the door in the landscape
Bottom: The door of the Corriere marks the beginning of the cycle and pedestrian path

Top: The river frontage of Travata
Bottom left: Southwest view of the route
Bottom right: The door of the Georgics stands out in the landscape
Opposite: Detail of the seat and the totem information

Jezzine Barracks

Location: Townsville, Australia
Area: 15 hectares (37 acres)
Landscape Design: Place Design Group
Photography: Andrew Rankin and Place Design Group
Client: Townsville City Council and Jezzine Barracks Community Trust

Jezzine Barracks is a 37-acre (15-hectare) site north of Townsville, Australia. The traditional custodians of the land are the Bindal and Wulgurukaba people, and the Australian Defence Force used the area for military accommodation and as a barracks for over 120 years. Thanks to the handover of the land by the Department of Defence, the site has now been transformed into public parkland.

One of the key successes of Jezzine Barracks is how it commemorates the Aboriginal and military heritage of the Kissing Point headland. A historical fort was left intact, with gentle architectural embellishments added to create greater access to gun emplacements and associated structures. The fort setting provides not only a wealth of interpretive elements but also a magnificent vantage point from which to enjoy the surrounding vistas. The stories of battles won and lost, as well as the creation story, are relayed through interpretive art pieces that allow the public to interact with the site and gain a sense of what it was once like.

Flowing paths link the various lookouts with views over the ocean to Magnetic Island and back over Townsville and the surrounding mountain ranges. The project design features an amphitheater, recreational facilities, boardwalks, bridges, and pedestrian paths, and incorporates bioretention drainage systems, which not only capture stormwater runoff but also provide natural boundaries

between key sections of the site. The natural terrain and the layout of the landscape design provide a range of public spaces that enables the site accessible to all, and for both passive and active recreational pursuits.

The Jezzine Barracks redevelopment has provided both the local and wider community with an enormous range of opportunities to interact with the site on various levels, encouraging pride in the local community and attracting visitors from throughout Australia and overseas.

Top: Crossed Boomerang Amphitheatre
Opposite top: View down to Garabarra Lawn
Opposite bottom: Bioretention drainage swale

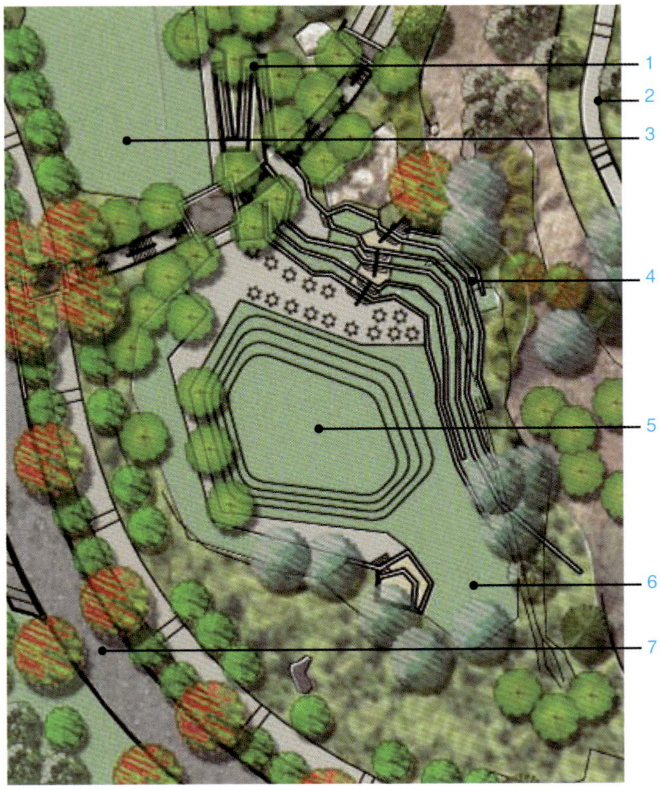

8

9

10

Crossed Boomerang Amphitheatre

1. Disabled ramp access to amphitheater
2. Walkway
3. Open space with markings of historic building location
4. Amphitheatrer terrace seating carved into existing embankment
5. Grass stage space
6. Views from peninsular back to Castle Hill
7. Jezzine Way and pedestrian walk
8. Amphitheater inspiration
9. Ampithearter stone wall backdrop
10. Terraced seating

Top: Evening View of Kennedy Regiment Plaza
Opposite top: Kissing Point Fort Arrival Plaza

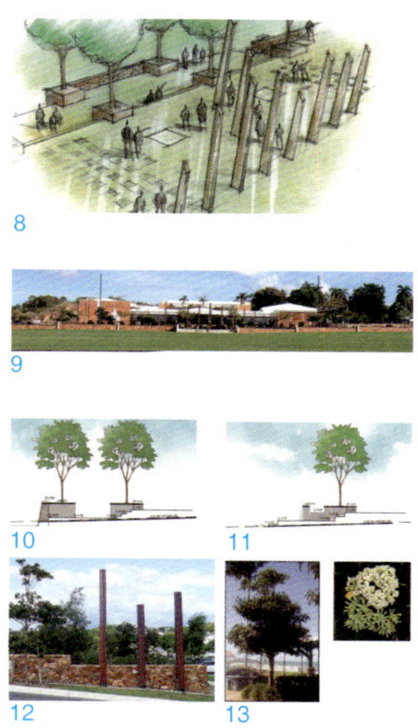

Kennedy Regiment Plaza

1. Military museum
2. Kennedy Regiment Plaza
3. Colonade of shade trees over plaza
4. Jezzine Way defined by bollards
5. Lower presentation platform overlooking parade ground open space
6. Taxi & bus parking
7. Viewing mound
8. Parade ground interpretive totems
9. Feature stone wall fronting Parade Ground
10. Section through stone wall
11. Section through terrace steps
12. Feature stone treatment
13. Feature plaza tree

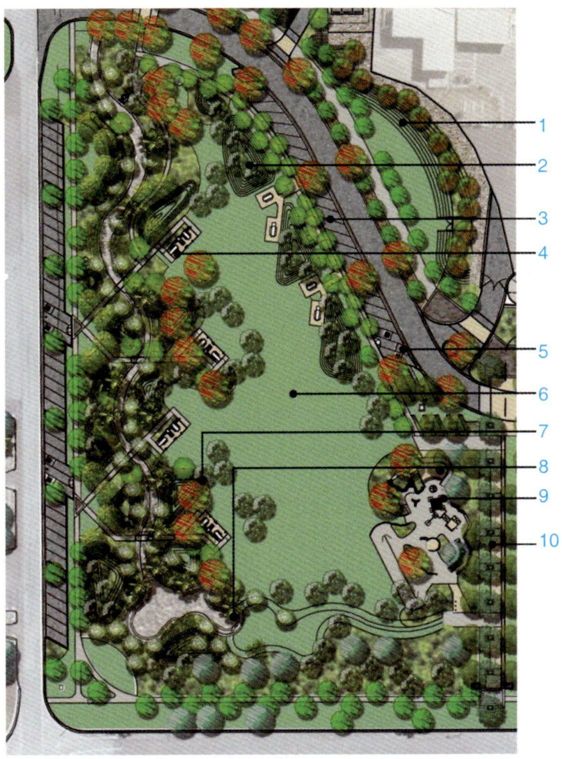

11

12

13

14

15

16

Norman Park

1. Mounded planting to buffer museum
2. Mounding to disguise parking beyond
3. Angled parking
4. Picnic shelter
5. Disability parking
6. Open space parkland
7. Native parkland setting
8. Bioretention pond
9. Playground with military theme
10. Pedestrian arrival plaza
11. Pedestrian access through parkland
12. Dry creek through native parkland
13. Timber bridge over dry creek
14. Gum trees used throughout parkland
15. Melaleuca used along dry creek
16. Bioretention pond set in native parkland

8

9

10

Community Precinct

1. Connection to coastal walk
2. Turnaround plaza sits below the fort and provides parking and viewing opportunities across Rowes Bay and up to the Palm group of islands
3. Service vehicle driveway access
4. Stair access to fort
5. Parking lot
6. Pedestrian walkways supported by gabion walls
7. Historic huts restored for community use
8. Pedestrian walkways up Kissing Point Hill provide all abilities access to historic fort
9. View to coastal walk connection
10. Stair access to Kissing Point Fort

Top: Walkway access up Boulder Garden Hill
Opposite top: Bill Coolburra Lookout overlooking Magnetic Island

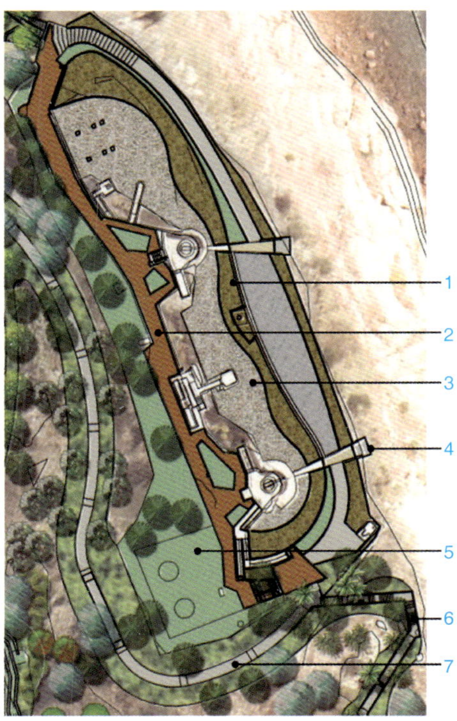

10

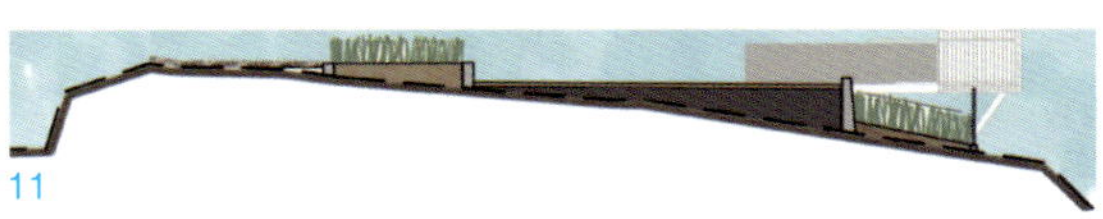
11

12

13

Kissing Point Fort

1. Terraced native grass buffer to top of fort
2. Brick paving adjacent to heritage structures
3. Gravel cover over top of fort
4. Observation lookouts aligned with guns
5. Turfed parade ground
6. Stepped boardwalk from jezzine entry
7. Pedestrian walkway from lower parkland
8. Kissing Point lookout
9. Sound and light show
10. Section through path and stone wall
11. Section through observation point
12. *Battle of the Coral Sea* artwork
13. Dry stacked stone wall

Top: Kissing Point Fort Arrival Plaza Lookout overlooking Magnetic Island
Opposite top: Jezzine Barracks Arrival Plaza

9

10

11

12

13

14

Ethno-Botanical Trail and Coastal Walk

1. Ethno-botanical trail
2. Coastal walk connection along the cliff face overlooking Rowes Bay
3. Garabarra lookout display and interpretive area
4. Natural hillside landscape
5. Seasonality ribbon
6. Bill Coolburra lookout and shelter provides sweeping views of the surrounding landscape
7. Cook Street entry on Jezzine Way
8. Boulder garden
9. Garbul Ceremony interpretive sculpture
10. Sculptural interpretive elements
11. Garabarra Lookout
12. Botanical trail overlooking ethno-botanical plantings
13. Garabarra Lookout
14. Ethno-botanical trail

10

11

12

Jezzine Barracks Arrival Precinct

1. Kissing Point Hill
2. Jezzine Way
3. Entry statement at base of hill
4. Connection to fort via steps
5. Disability parking to service the Rock Pool precinct
6. Line of norfolk pines creates a vista to the entry statement
7. Parking lot to service Rock Pool and parkland precincts
8. Entry off the Strand and Howitt Street roundabout
9. Pedestrian arrival path
10. Entry military totems
11. Parking lot bioretention pond
12. Norfolk pines used as an entry feature

Top: Jezzine Way Timeline Walk
Opposite top: Movie night entertainment on the Parade Ground

7

8

9

10

11

Brigadier North Park

1. Jezzine Way
2. Parking lot off Jezzine Way
3. Bioretention pods serve function of stormwater treatment and protection of pedestrians from traffic
4. Open space
5. Pedestrian link through site
6. Bioretention pond surrounded by turf mounds
7. Bioretention pond set amongst stone walls
8. Bioretention swale beside Jezzine Way
9. Jezzine Way and pedestrian path feed into Bioretention swale
10. Feature shade trees along the road
11. Feature shade trees the along pedestrian path

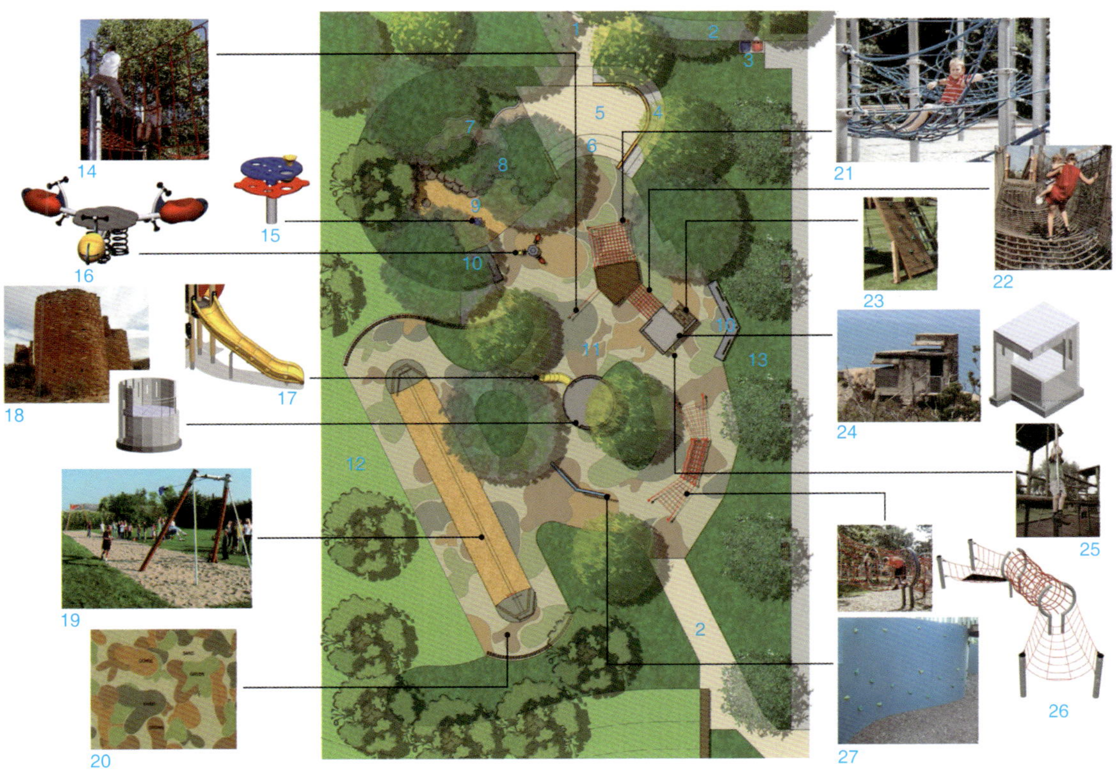

Proposed Military-Themed Playground

1. Bike racks
2. Path
3. Trash cans
4. Ramp
5. Arrival plaza
6. Steps
7. Adventure trail
8. Rocks
9. Junior play area
10. Seats
11. Military-themed area
12. Lawn
13. Plants
14. Vertical amusement net
15. Rotating sand play table
16. Triple unit spring toy 'blazer'
17. Slide
18. Custom fort
19. Flying fox
20. Softfall camouflage pattern
21. Quadrangle amusement net
22. Rope net bridge
23. Climbing ramp
24. Custom fort
25. Pole slide
26. Crawl net
27. Climbing wall

Top left: Access steps to Bill Coolburra Lookout
Top right: All abilities access through the ethno-botanical park
Bottom: *Wars* sculpture located at Kissing Point Fort
Opposite: Coastal walk along the cliff face

Park Groot Schijn, Zone Boterlaar Silsburg

Location: Antwerp, Belgium
Area: 6.5 hectares (16 acres)
Landscape Design: MAXWAN Architects + Urbanists
Photography: Filip Dujardin
Client: AG Stadsplanning Antwerpen

Maxwan Architects+Urbanists took on the entire park design for the Park Groot Schijn project, including landscaping (a qualitative improvement of the Koude Beek valley), the development of 172 community gardens and reservation of about 30 additional gardens, plus parking for around 50 cars.

Close to Antwerp, the location—set across 700,000 square feet (65,000 square meters)—shows unprecedented character, with the meandering Koude Beek as its iconic element.

The brief was to preserve and strengthen the landscape's existing qualities. To solve the site's water-management issues, terrain levels were subtly modified and four gullies were integrated in the landscape.

New garden complexes and river valleys were also integrated into the existing neighborhood, and appear as robust and clearly recognizable clusters in the landscape.

The path network gives access from five different spots, and connects all major locations, and provides a continuous range perspective. The landscape is at times wet and dry, so the vegetation is a mix of grasses and flowers that suit the habitat.

South Park Master Plan

South Park Master Plan

All the ingredients for an ecological, social, open, accessible, and attractive park are here, and the entire design meets the pre-established goals for an integrated spatial organization, including solutions for water management and a strong desire to make the park attractive for a wide range of users.

Top: The lush vegetation along the river

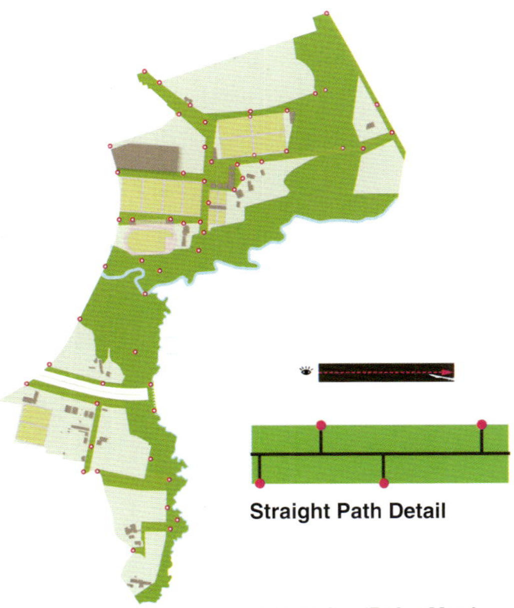

Straight Path Detail

Illustrative 'Point Map'
The path network connects all major 'points' in the park, including entrances and exists to buildings and fields, objects, and a scenic view of the valley

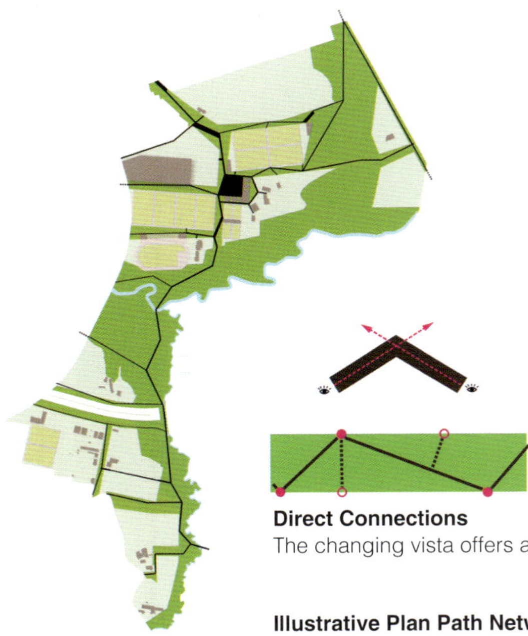

Direct Connections
The changing vista offers a diverse experience

Illustrative Plan Path Network
Such major 'points' are connected to become a coherent path network. By having no straight route, yet continuously bending and changing perspectives of the park, one can experience the intimacy and diversity of the surrounding vistas

Top: Masonry bridge across the river
Opposite top: Profile of the bridge

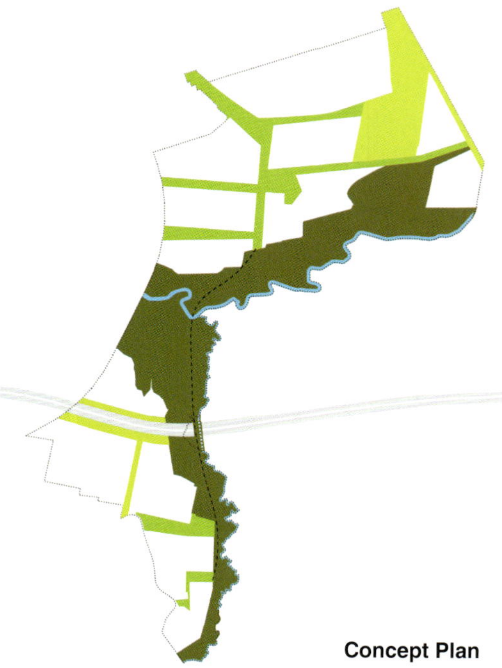

Concept Plan

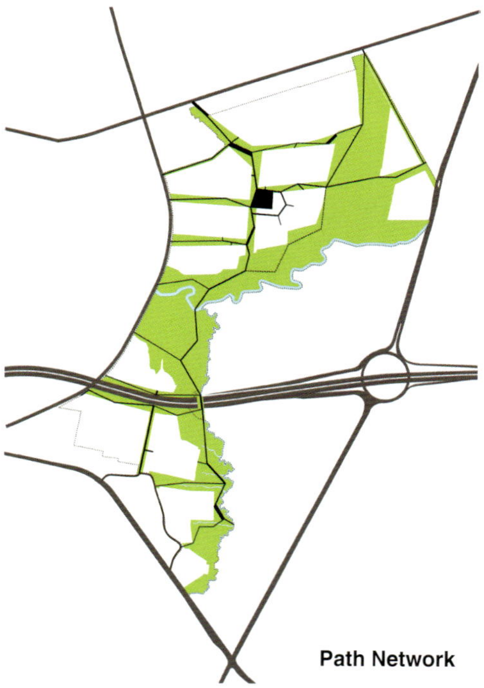

Path Network

Green Seams Valley Concept

Path Connections

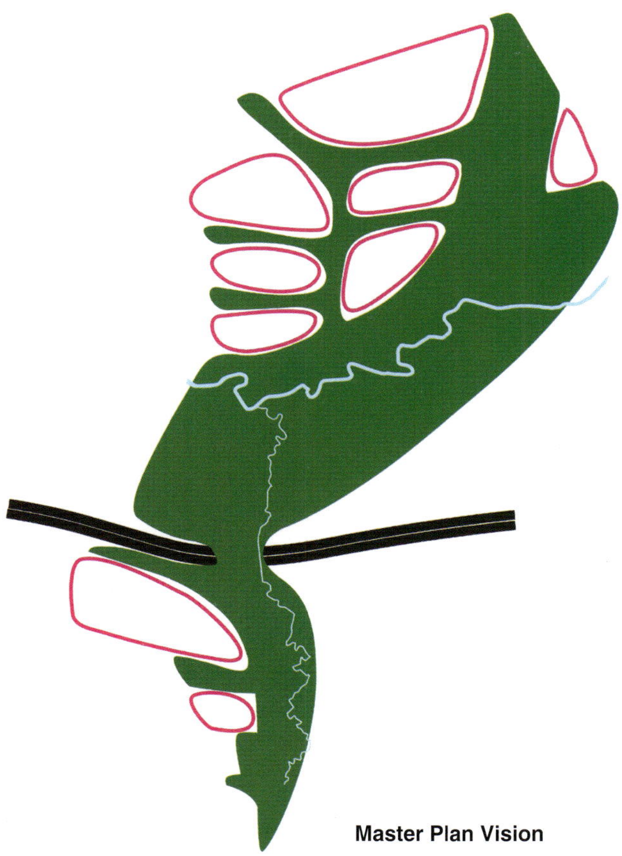

Master Plan Vision

Sketch

Top: White chairs and tables at the rest area
Opposite top: The winding river and the surrounding vegetation

Sketch

Sketch

Top: The winding river
Bottom: The lane surrounded by green vegetation
Opposite top: The red bridge across the river sits in stark contrast with the surrounding green lawn
Opposite bottom left: The logo of the park on the bridge
Opposite bottom right: The park name set in sculpture

Top: Vegetable garden huts
Bottom: Vegetables growing in the garden
Opposite: Flower beds next to the wooden fence

Mangfall Park

Location: Rosenheim, Bavaria, Germany
Area: 13 hectares (32 acres)
Landscape Design: A24 Landschaft Landschaftsarchitektur GmbH
Photography: Hanns Joosten
Client: LGS Rosenheim 2010 GmbH

Water management is becoming a growing factor in landscape architecture and urban design, and Mangfall Park in Germany is an excellent example of how both sustainable water management and sublime design can be accomplished in one project.

This new and highly-frequented recreation area, with multiple waterways, rivers, creeks, and an urban stream, contains bridges, boardwalks, and flood protection dikes as its chief design elements. To this end, the new park was given a backbone of three landscape boardwalks that cross the waterways and their embankments, connect the city to the parkland, and end in the natural landscape. The boardwalks, up to 630 feet (192 meters) long, simultaneously function as promenades, ramps, bridges, viewpoints, seats, and lounging areas. They also allow movement in new directions: where people once strolled along individual waterways, they can now crisscross the various rivers and dikes, one after the next. The crossings add new dimensions to the waterways, and also negotiate the differences in height between the dikes and the flatland, enabling barrier-free access to the area.

The spacious northern section of the park extends the city's open spaces to the Inn River. This expansive parkland flows into the vastness of the river landscape. The linear waterway motif is thus carried to the newly formulated city edge, and new access points

offer passageways to the city. An entrance square marks the beginning of the northern park, and the Promenade Boardwalk proceeds from the square to the junction of the Mangfall and Inn rivers, where it deeply juts into the river mouth and offers a view to the Bavarian Alps.

As opposed to the spacious northern park, with its serene waterways that unite visitors with nature, the southern park is a denser area with capacity for a variety of recreational sports and children's activities. A flood protection dike divides the southern park into a more artificial, regulated park along the Hammerbach and Mangfall River basins, with its fluctuating water levels and naturalistic landscape. Shallow banks enable access to the Mangfall River itself. The main attractions in the southern park are the kayak course and a play area for children. This area is connected to surrounding sports and recreational facilities by a boardwalk, creating barrier-free access and a continuous play and recreational area.

The piped streambed of the Mühlbach River has been exposed and devised as an attractive green corridor. Located between a planned high-end residential area on the grounds of a former factory, an existing power station, and the inner-city, the Mühlbach River connects this new neighborhood with the city center and the river landscape, allowing for the development of attractive green spaces close to residential units. In contrast to the natural setting, the Mühlbach River is designed as an 'urban stream,' located in the inner city and visibly contained within retaining walls, whereby inlets create space for urban gardens.

Mangfall Park has become an engine for urban renewal in adjacent neighborhoods. It is frequently visited and has become a popular recreation area close to the city center. The project has enjoyed worldwide publicity and received honorable mentions and prizes on an international level.

Top: The old and new river dikes not only offer flood protection, but are also characteristic elements of the park's design. A 13-foot (4 meter) high and 1-mile (1.6 kilometer) long dike divides the park into an urban park landscape and the Mangfall River basin with its fluctuating water-level and typical plants

Opposite top: The boardwalks cross the waterways and connect the city to the new parkland and the Inn River. The boardwalks function simultaneously as promenades, ramps, bridges, viewpoints, seats, and lounging areas

Detail plan promenade boardwalk with entrance square

Top: The integration of the park into the wetlands results in diverse intersections with the riverbanks. Sometimes dramatic, sometimes subdued, they carve out the different qualities of these junctions of land and water

The Promenade Boardwalk, 630-feet (192 meters) long, leads from the opening square to the Inn Balcony and ends in a 26 foot (8 meter) protruding platform

The Mangfall Boardwalk crosses the Hammerbach and the Mangfall River and ends in the natural landscape on Inn Island

Nicklwiesen Boardwalk runs through the southern park, crosses the embankments of the Mangfall and ends in the existing recreational area

Top: The boardwalks provide barrier-free access to the park area and the surrounding landscape. The bridges have a steel construction with sculptured columns

Bottom: The different gardens along the Hammerbach—Perennial Garden, Cloud Garden, Giant Garden, Driftwood Garden, and Fern Garden—combine a sensual experience

Top: In contrast to the natural setting of the other waterways, the unpiped Mühlbach is felt as an 'urban stream' set in the inner city, and is visibly contained within retaining walls. Inlets create space for urban stream gardens along the water. The green corridor now connects the new urban housing development, the inner city, and the river landscape
Bottom: Stream gardens, like the Flamingo Garden with its shrubbery and seating, offer ample room to spend time near the water. The geometry of the garden beds trace the movements of the stream. A long bench invites the visitors to sit in the sun while enjoying the view of the Mühlbach
Opposite top: This thin, waning end of a peninsula is the most remote corner of the park. A picturesque stone mound with simple seating stages the confluence of the Inn and Mangfall, where the rivers' differently hued waters flow together
Opposite bottom: The course of the Hammerbach has become a kayak route for children. Large gravel islands made of concrete have a dynamic effect on the stream, creating an exciting mix of wider and narrower sections of the riverbed

Botanical Garden of Faial

Location: Horta, Portugal
Area: 3350 square meters (36059 square feet)
Landscape Design: Topiaris Landscape Architecture
Photography: João Morgado Architectural Photography
Client: Regional Government of Azores

The Botanical Garden of Faial, located on Faial Island, around 1 mile (2 kilometers) from the city of Horta in Portugal, is widely referenced as having one of the world's best collections of Macaronesian flora, with a notably unique and rare collection. Set in a valley, the location offers outstanding views and excellent conditions for the installation of native species and habitats of the Azores archipelago.

Topiaris were engaged in a redevelopment project intended to value the botanical garden as a whole. The growing number of visitors demanded a strategy to rehabilitate the existing park in its landscape and botanical dimensions, and develop a new concept for the area in terms of the exhibition of traditional botanic species. The design uses a contemporary language to recreate the dynamics of the local ecosystem. It also reinterprets the natural and cultural land features of each taxonomy present in the archipelago, such as morphology, altitude, proximity to the sea, trees, and territorial cultural patterns, adding more interest for visitors.

The botanical garden is composed of three homogenous zones: an area with buildings, an arboretum, and an area for herbs, ferns, and bryophytes. Stone walls were designed for the rehabilitation areas, together with the introduction of traditional farm crops, medicinal plants, and invasive and Azorean gardens plants, aiming to expand the potential of the garden.

Top: The herb garden was inspired by local volcanic land forms, with the volcanic Mount Pico (almost 6561 feet/2000 meters high) in the background

The new areas developed by Topiaris adopt an organic design, inspired by volcanic geomorphology in the Azores. Traditional materials have been used, allowing full continuity between the old and new gardens. New elements were also introduced, including a native tree and shrub border; site grading performing elevations or depressions; and basalt stone walls and paths, which enclose particular thematic areas and allow comfortable conditions for observation and interpretation of the botanical collection.

The contemporary design introduces boundaries for different areas. While respecting the role of a traditional botanical garden, it also embraces leadership in its preparation for future challenges.

Top: Access to the fern garden is via stairs made from local basalt stone slabs
Bottom left: The vision for the park was inspired by local volcanic land forms
Bottom right: Natural basalt blocs are used along the walkways

Top: The pattern of hills and depressions enabled the design of a winding path , increasing interest for visitors

View of the Circular Area, Designed to Recreate a Coastal Habitat

1. Orchidarium
2. Traditional farmland, citrus trees, sugarcane, tea, tobacco
3. Invasive plants
4. Medicinal and aromatic plants
5. Ornamental Azorean plants
6. Azorean laurisilva (laurel forest)
7. Coastal laurisilva (laurel forest)
8. Rocky benches habitat
9. Endemic Macaronesian shrub habitats
10. Coastal wetlands
11. Sand and dunes habitats
12. Ferns and bryophytes
13. Medium altitude herbaceous
14. Herbaceous wetlands habitats and bogs
15. Highland herbaceous habitats

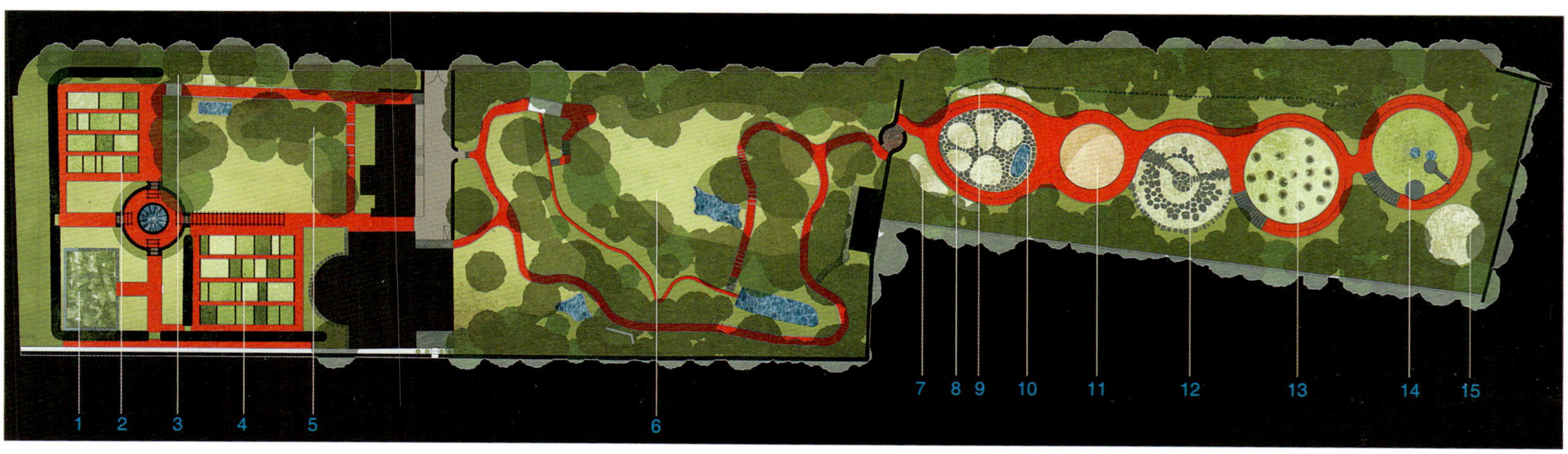

Top: Overall garden plan showing the three main areas of plant collection (from left to right): a) orthogonal pattern with fragrant, medicinal, agriculture, ornamental and invasive plants; b) heaving pattern of the arboretum; c) circular patterns of the endemic herbaceous area

Construction Detail for the High-Altitude Moss Wetlands

1. Groundwater
2. Free water surface
3. Waterproofing
4. Planting substract (sphagnum bog)
5. Basalt rocks

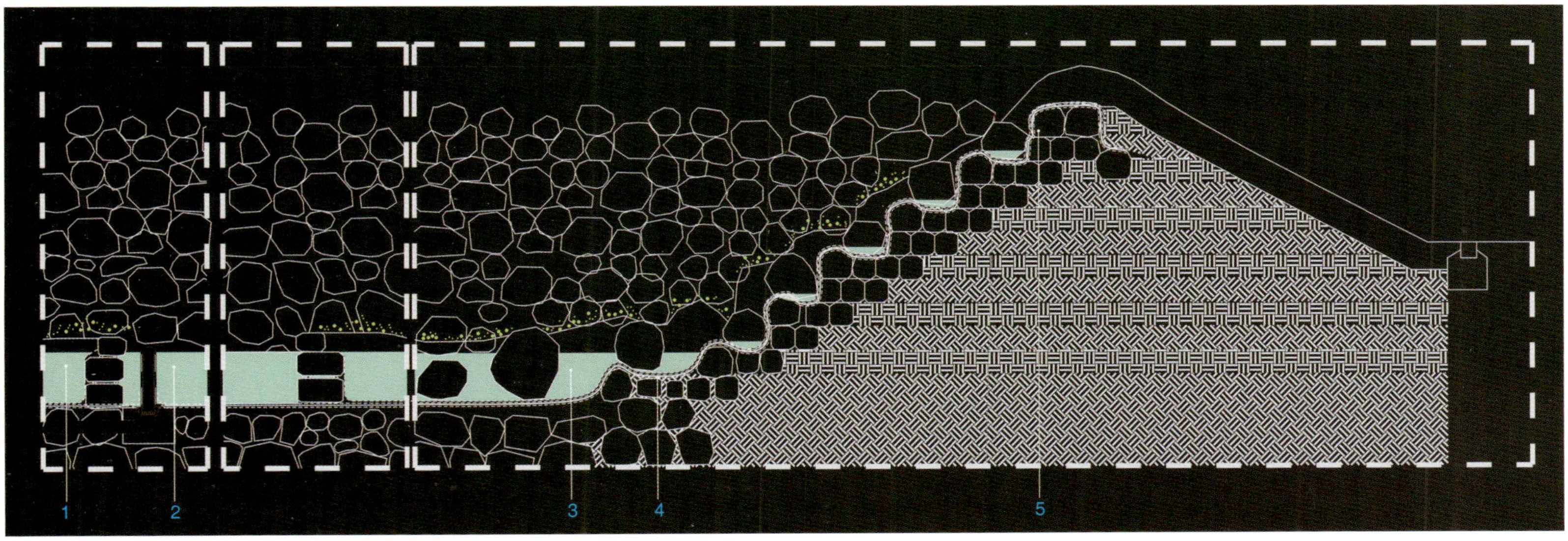

Top: Basalt stone walls divisions in an agricultural species area
Bottom: Basalt stone wall divisions in a fragrant species area
Opposite top: Mirror water feature under pergola of wisteria
Opposite bottom: Water tank in the area for displaying introduced by man botanic species: ornamental and invasive

Edmondson Park

Location: Edmondson Park, Sydney, Australia
Area: 6 hectares (14.83 acres)
Landscape Design: Sturt Noble Associates
Photography: Sturt Noble Associates
Client: UrbanGrowth NSW

Sturt Noble Associates was engaged to create a master plan and design all landscaping elements for a new residential estate in outer suburban Sydney. This encompassed all open space areas, including the development of three new parks—Bardia Park, Brigade Park, and Valley Reserve.

The design team also developed the entire estate experience, including the main entry, sales office, streetscapes, and design treatments for medium-density housing.

Brigade Park is designed as a native bushland landscape intended for high levels of activity, and therefore integrates a fitness circuit, adventure playground, walking trails, and a primary pedestrian commuter path. The lower part of the park also accommodates a barbecue area, shelters, and seating, as well a large lawn area.

Bardia Park is designed as a welcome to the residents of the estate, and features a large entry with a feature wall and a significant fig tree.

Valley Reserve is a free, unstructured space for local residents. Safe and protected informal paths take walkers on a journey through an open woodland setting, and an off-leash dog walking area is also provided.

Public art has been integrated into the parks, with artwork based on commemorative military medals and ribbons decorating glazed brick feature walls and painted totems.

Site Plan

Top: Raised planter
Opposite top: Recycled bricks are integrated into paving

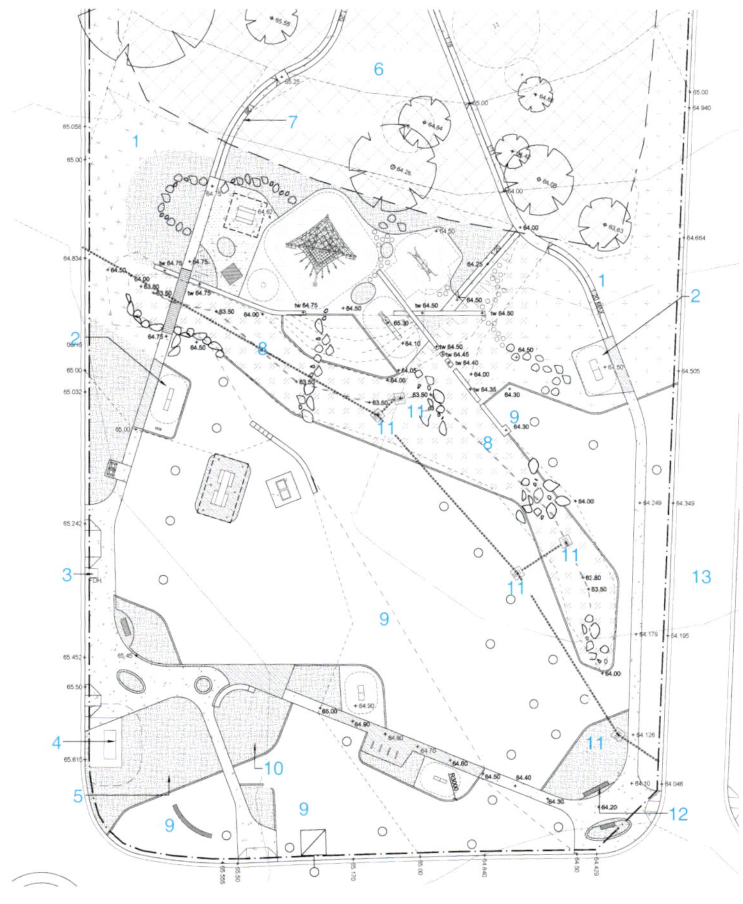

Site Plan

1. Revegetation area
2. Fitness area
3. Location of TFAN to be confirmed by engineer
4. Proposed substation
5. Feature wall
6. Sympathetic management of cumnerland park woodland as per edmondson park conservation agreement
7. Concrete footpath
8. Overland flow
9. Lawn
10. Native ornamental planting bed
11. Top of pit
12. Feature wall
13. Road

Top: Bicycle racks, drinking fountain, and recycled brick paving
Opposite top: Concrete and recycled brick paving

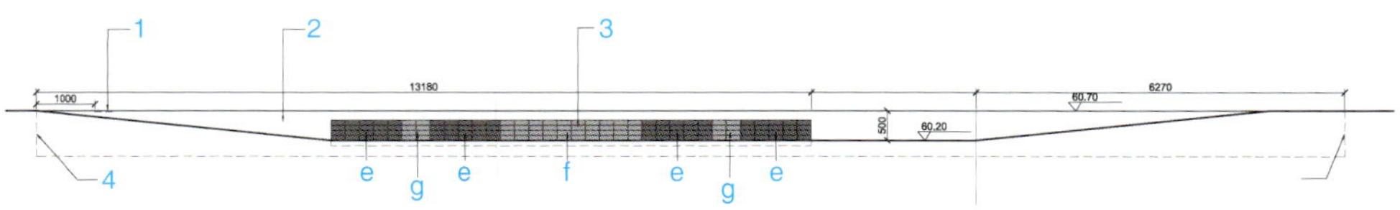

Scale 1:50

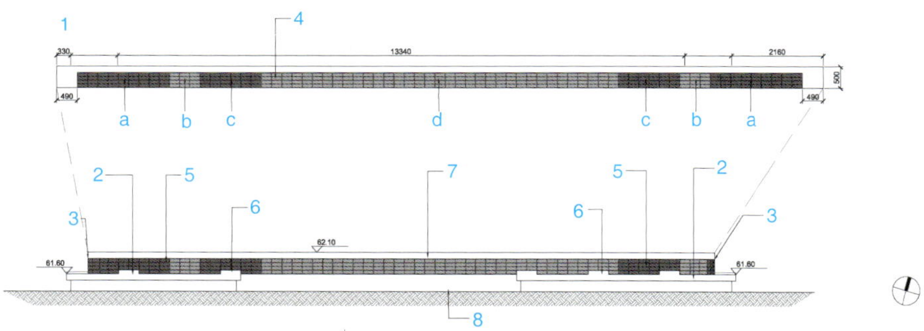

Scale 1:50

Note: Paint color for ribbons is referenced from *The Significance of Ribbon Colours on Medals Worn Since 1815 by Australians* by Rick Grebert (Landers Publishing, 2007).

Elevation 1

1. Plaque to top surface
2. Concrete/brick wall
3. Glazed brick representation of the 'Africa Star' medal ribbon
4. End of wall

a. Blue
b. Black
c. White
d. Orange
e. Beige
f. Red
g. Navy blue

Elevation 2

1. Seat back extent elevation
2. Concrete seating wall
3. Continues around corner as above
4. Glazed brick representation of the 'British War Medal' ribbon
5. Glazed brick infill
6. Raised concrete form to stop skate grinding
7. Concrete retaining wall
8. Adjacent lawn falls west to east

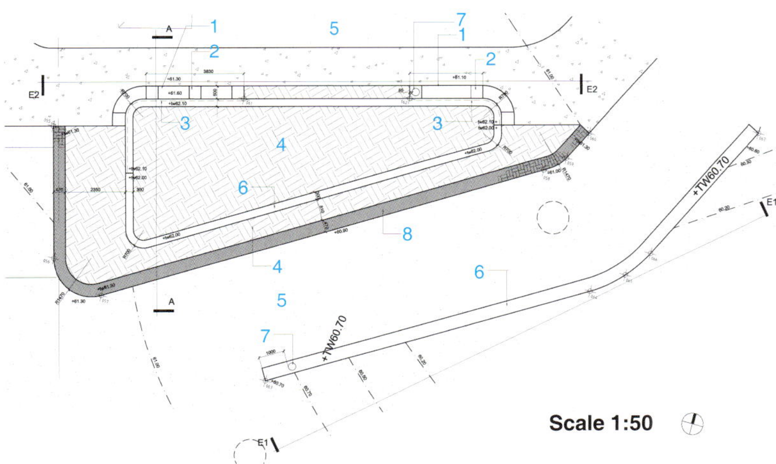

Scale 1:50

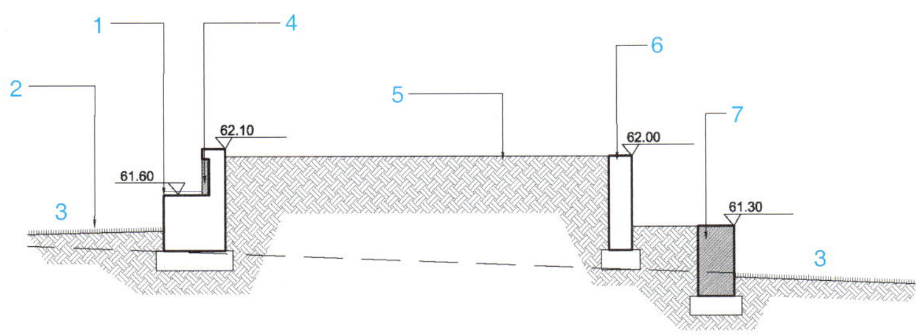

Scale 1:50

Detail Plan

1. Concrete seating wall
2. Raised concrete form to stop skate grinding
3. Location of glazed brick infill
4. Concrete retaining wall
5. Lawn area
6. Planting area
7. Plaque to top surface
8. Recycled brick retaining wall

Section

1. Concrete seating wall
2. Lawn area
3. Adjacent Lawn area
4. Glazed brick infill
5. Planting area
6. Concrete retaining wall
7. Recycled brick retaining wall

Top: Seating walls with military ribbon colors
Bottom: Banksia garden
Opposite top: Picnic shelter on recycled brick paving
Opposite bottom left: Totems with military ribbon colors
Opposite bottom right: Water-sensitive reec gardens with interactive children play elements

Tagus Linear Park

Location: Póvoa de Santa Iria, Portugal
Area: 15 hectares (37 acres)
Landscape Design: Topiaris Landscape Architecture
Photography: João Morgado
Client: Municipality of Vila Franca de Xira

The Tagus Linear Park is an area of 161,458 square feet (15,000 square meters) and was developed so that surrounding communities could have access to the Tagus River.

For the first time, residents of the adjacent urban communities have been given recreation and leisure opportunities in an area that was previously blocked by large industrial lots. Visitors are now invited to enjoy the landscape and a diverse array of equipment and activities, from sports, fishing, walking, and cycling to environmental education.

The objective for the park was to rethink urban public space in a complex industrial and agricultural area. Aiming to keep the essence of the area, the design team created a unique greenway, incorporating the landscape's natural and cultural features alongside a multitude of recreational and leisure options, safeguarding the existing natural systems and promoting the ecological regeneration of damaged areas.

The park combines two different spaces: a single multifunctional area named Praia dos Pescadores (Fisherman's Beach), set by the riverside within a former sand deposit, and around 4 miles (6 kilometers) of pedestrian trails. The connection between the 'beach' and the natural areas is made via a 2296-foot (700-meter) long

Top: Aerial photograph of Fisherman's Beach showing natural vegetation clusters used in the landscape design, and and nearby industry, abandoned, and natural farmland areas

raised wooden path, from which a bird observation deck built from old pallets can be reached.

Praia dos Pescadores contains a set of diverse and complementary equipment primarily intended for environmental education, leisure, and informal sports, and includes fishing platforms and shelters, picnic areas, a volleyball court, and a playground made from recycled tires, as well as platforms for sunbathing, creating an interesting and unique area. The name was inspired by the local fishermen, who were skeptical of the project at the beginning but soon realized the renovated space would keep the same sense of place that they had always been attracted to. Their constant presence proved to be a sustainable and efficient surveillance strategy.

Lighting throughout the park is also 100 percent solar powered, and a center for environmental and landscape education was also constructed for housing temporary exhibitions and events. It was built in a modular system using recycled maritime containers, and its structure is slightly raised from the ground, generating a spatial pattern that takes advantage of the views toward the ecosystems nearby.

A network of paths, made from concrete slabs, defines the main spatial structure and connects all components of the park. Vegetation is composed mainly of native species and was planted in clusters, creating a specific formal pattern that contrasts with the extensive sand area.

A mesh of individual wooden poles that help capture and secure sand protects the densely planted groups, and also shields plants from being trampled on in their early stages of development.

Fisherman's Beach Layout Plan

1. Maritime facilities
2. Picnic area
3. Sand
4. Marshland
5. Entry
6. Playground
7. Fishing shelter
8. Fishing platform
9. Parking
10. Showers
11. Stage for events
12. Solar lamp
13. Beach voley ball court
14. Old maritime tools as sculptures
15. Solariums
16. Povoa's trail
17. Link to urban park and urban areas
18. Wooden fence
19. Solar panels
20. Cafeteria
21. Rest rooms
22. Center for Environmental and Landscape Interpretation
23. Concrete slabs
24. Mesh of wooden beams to protect native species
25. Fishing platforms/ancient pier
26. Recovered marshland
27. Canico's Stream
28. Farmland
29. Stream's banks restoration
30. Drainage ditch
31. Bridge
32. Tagus's Trail
33. Links to natural areas
34. Marshland
35. Tagus river

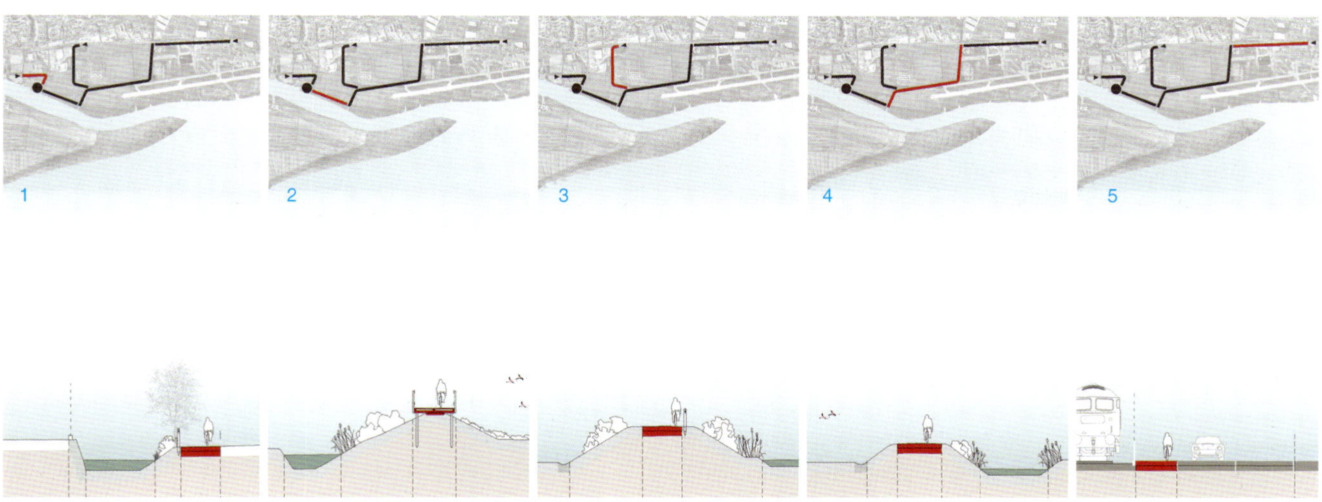

Trail Sections

1. Povoa's Trail
2. Tagus's Trail
3. Forte da Casa's Trail
4. Verdelha's Trail
5. Estacao's Trail

Top: Upper view toward the Tagus River, including a beach volleyball court surrounded by natural vegetation
Opposite top: Upper view toward the Tagus River featuring orthogonal concrete paths with clusters of natural vegetation and a playground with recycled tires
Opposite bottom: Upper view toward upstream, with a picnic area and wood pavement

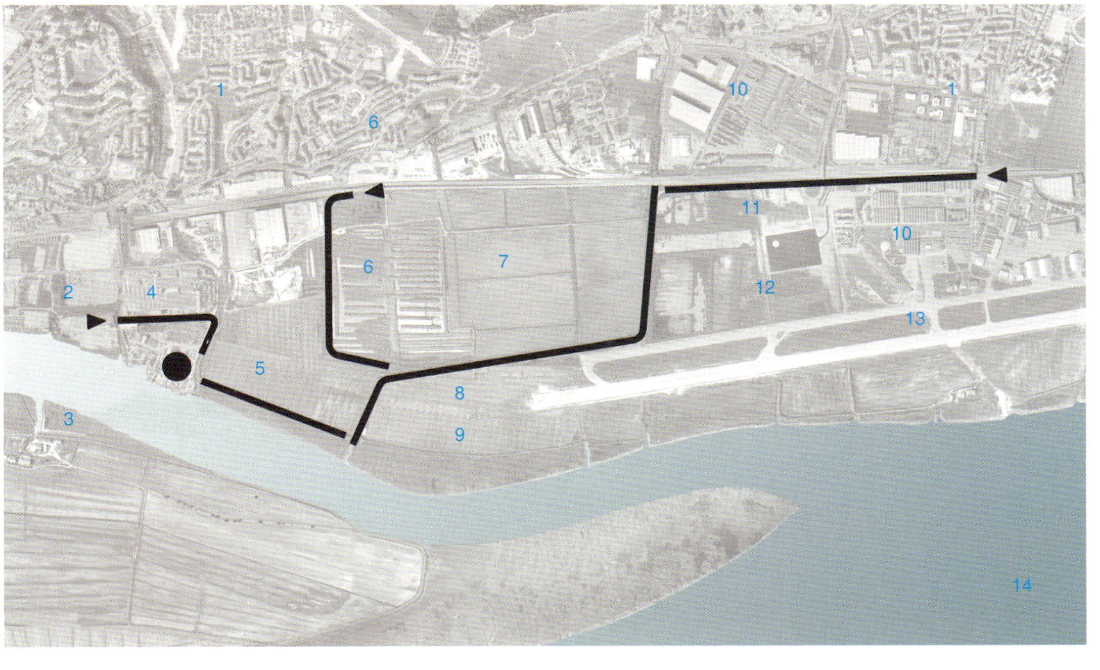

Map Location

1. Urban area
2. Urban park
3. Fisherman's Beach
4. Povoa's Trail
5. Tagus's Trail
6. Forte da Casa's Trail
7. Farmland
8. Verdelha's Trail
9. Saltmarsh
10. Industrial area
11. Estacao's Trail
12. Abandoned salt ponds
13. Military facility
14. Tagus River

Top: Wooden fishing shelters along the riverbank
Bottom: Natural vegetation along the river margins, between concrete platforms designed for fishing
Opposite top: Shaded wooden seating areas
Opposite bottom: Seating areas

trilho
do
tejo

Top and bottom: Bird watch shelters made from recycled wood pallets
Opposite top: Wooden deck path
Opposite bottom left: Wooden deck path
Opposite bottom right: View over wetlands and river

Top: View over wetlands and river
Bottom: Linear concrete path and vegetation clusters
Opposite: Vegetation clusters surrounded by different wooden fences; the Interpretation Centre in the background is made from recycled shipping containers

Top: Loose pavement in crushed limestone separate the natural areas and farmland
Bottom: Path along farmland limits, separated by wooden poles
Opposite top: Wooden beams along the path
Opposite bottom: Rest areas along the path

Parc François Mitterrand

Location: Cergy-Pontoise, France
Area: 8 hectares (19.77 acres)
Landscape Design: URBICUS Ltd/Jean-Marc Gaulier
Project Manager: Rudy Blanc
Photography: Charles Delcourt, Katarina Sambroska, Bernard Moreau
Client: Communauté d'aAgglomération de Cergy-Pontoise

Originally designed in 1974 by Alain Provost, the Parc François Mitterrand—once a breath of fresh area in the local area—had become a little-known spot, disconnected from expanding Cergy-Pontoise. To address this, in 2009 the Agglomeration Community of Cergy-Pontoise decided to launch a vast program of works to regenerate the park. The park's restoration, completed in 2013 by URBICUS, has opened it up to local amenities (such as the nearby university), businesses (including restaurants and cafes), and the surrounding neighborhoods.

Redevelopment of the park was designed to respect the environment and is in keeping with the sustainable management of the area. The main challenge was for the redevelopment to carefully fit in with existing tree coverage in the park. A very detailed inventory of the existing vegetation was made, and every remarkable tree preserved and showcased in the redevelopment.

The park's functions were also reorganized. Large meadows, which contribute to the diversification and enrichment of the park's biodiversity, were sustained, and new flowerbeds introduced, offering rich, diversified new biotopes. The Grande Place (main square) and Pelouses Récréatives (a grassed recreation area) were added and offer places for contemplation and rest, and encourage people in the community to come together.

Furniture was changed to create a modern look that suits the park's new image. A wooden promenade runs along the spillway channel and turns into a sundeck. Here, users can sit on custom-made wooden seats in the sun or shade. The wooden deck ends in a belvedere above the pond, and visitors can feel as if they are walking on water, and can watch the waterfowl that have acclimatized to this new environment.

The use of wood is clearly in evidence throughout the park and reinforces the environmentally-friendly image. The wood varieties used are PEFC-certified and come from French forests.

The project offered an opportunity to completely overhaul the structure and sealing of the park's ponds, which have been divided into three new biozones. The banks of the ponds were planted with wetland vegetation, and lagooning zones have been formed to enable phyto-purification of the park's water. This in turn encourages certain bird species to nest there. The regeneration zone is made up of purifying plants such as Phalaris arundinacea (reed canarygrass), Pontederia cordata (pickerelweed), Juncus effuses (common rush), Iris pseudacorus (yellow iris), Lythrum salicaria (purple loosestrife), and Caltha palustris (marsh marigold), which help to filter the water. Filtering is also performed by a pump system that sends the water into a UV sand filter. This removes tenacious algae, which is harmful to the pond's biodiversity.

Oxygenation is provided by a spillway channel of around 492 feet (150 meters) in length, with projections to stir and oxygenate the water. Some of the purified water from the sand filter is sent to the top of a waterfall and some is sent directly to the ponds via a Venturi effect sluice gate system.

Top: The wooden walkway finishes in a pontoon above the pond
Opposite top: The banks of the pondy

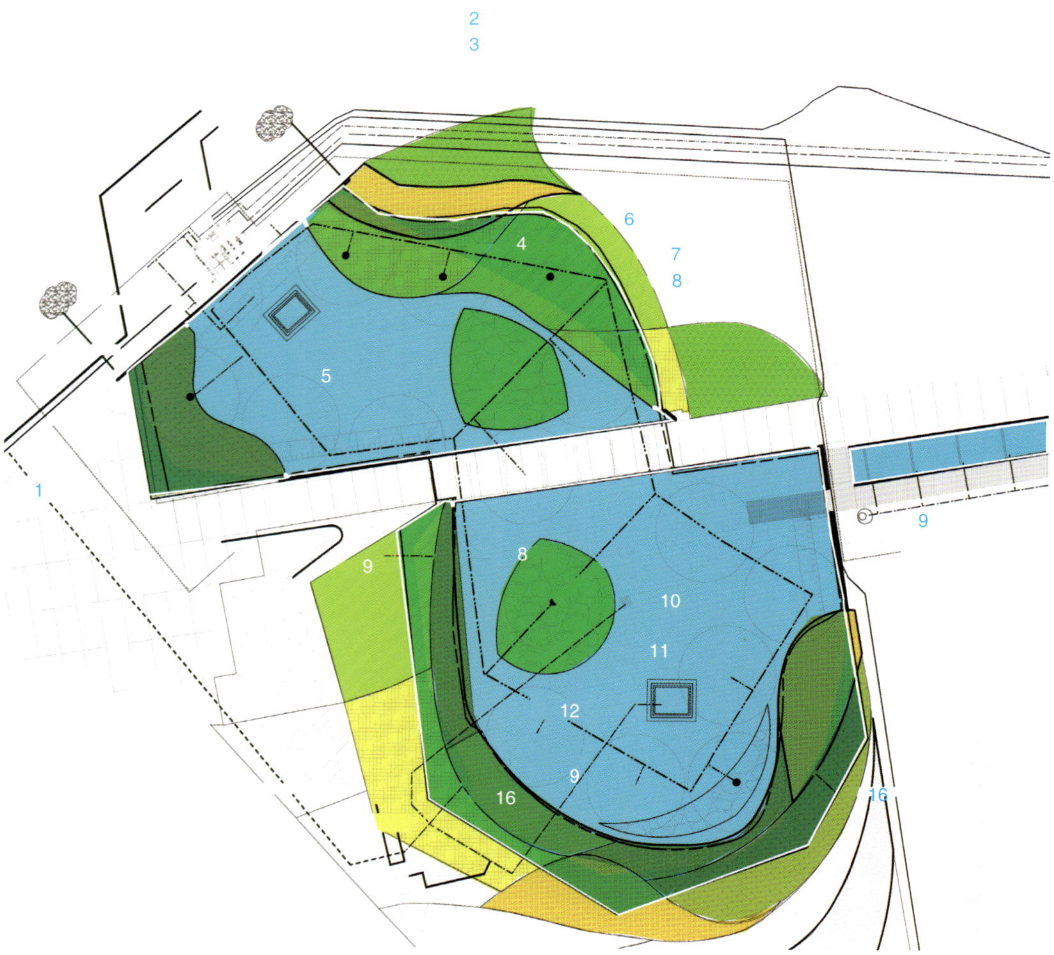

Functional Zoning Map

1. Connection to the existing network
2. Watering of the northern part
3. Watering of the south part
4. Filtration network
5. Approval pond north
6. Low wall
7. Anchoring of the waterproof ness
8. Water level
9. Emptying
10. Existing emptying
11. Pit for ashes
12. Level of stop
13. Bottom of the pond
14. Emptying
15. Gate
16. Overflow DN 150

Top: View of the pond
Middle: The existing trees were preserved and integrated into the project
Bottom: Walking paths
Oppposite top: Multi-use path and vegetation

Top: A wooden terrace offers a path along the canal
Bottom: Wood has been used to build the terrace and seating areas
Oppposite top: A grassed provides a space for games and relaxing
Oppposite bottom: Areas of undergrowth

Le Syndrome de la Page Blanche

Location: Amiens, France
Area: 1500 square meters (16146 square feet)
Landscape Design: Les Jardiniers Nomades
Photography: Les Jardiniers Nomades
Client: Maison de la Culture d'Amiens

A stone's throw from the center of Amiens lays the Hortillonnages, an area of unique gardens set in a world heritage destination. Reclaimed from ancient marshland, this vast 'floating garden' is made up of a network of canals surrounding cultivated islands. This remarkable man made landscape has experienced a slow evolution over the centuries, but fell into decline in the early 2000s. Faced with extinction of the islands due to erosion, members of the local community mobilized to save this area.

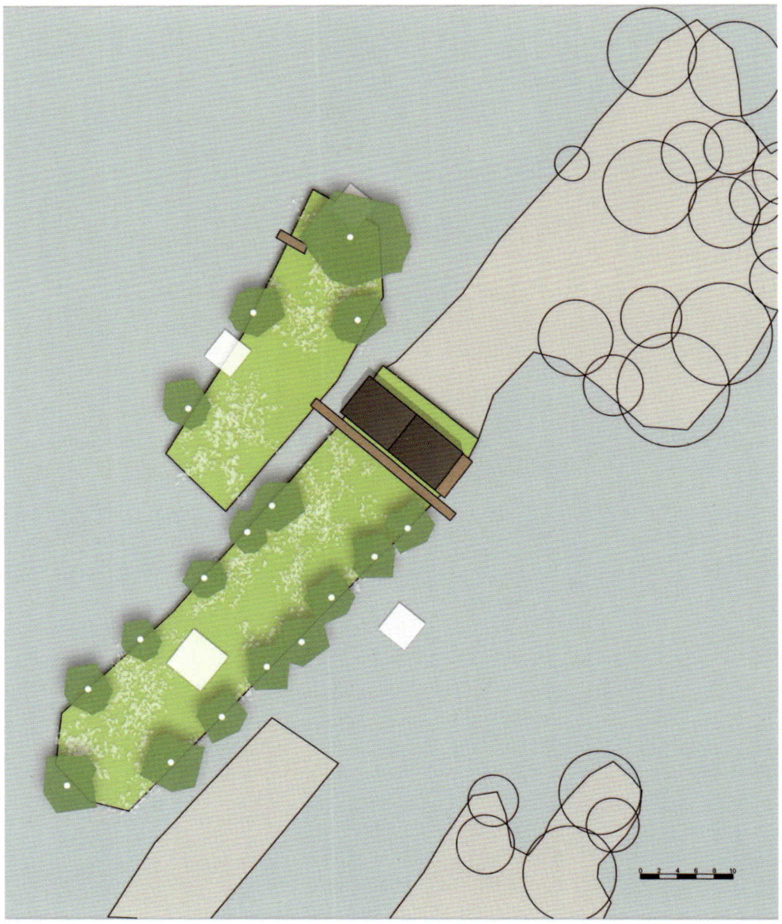

In 2010 the Maison de la Culture d'Amiens launched its first cultural festival, with the aim of attracting visitors to the Hortillonnages and inform and educate through the intervention of young architects, artists, and landscape architects.

Les Jardiniers Nomades were selected to develop an attraction for the festival. A neglected island dominated by a hut in ruins lay at the heart of the Hortillonnages, and the design team was drawn to this location, seduced by the inherent symbolic reference to a landscape in decline. The project, le Syndrome de la Page Blanche ('syndrome of the blank page'), didn't take the island as a basis for a work of art, but rather saw it as a work of art in its own right.

The work Les Jardiniers Nomades undertook on the island characterizes the Hortillonnages and its different components,

namely: the exceptional fertile nature of the soil, which is illustrated by the abundance of the wild meadows on the island; the trees that spontaneously appear, revealing the architectural strength of nature; the hut, sober and mysterious, which is open on one side and acts as a 'camera obscura' from which the observer can appreciate the apparent tranquility of the water and the illusion of a constant landscape; and the plenitude offered by this remarkable environment, which is put at the hand of the observer thanks to big wooden structures that invite visitors to meditate in the hollow of a net, suspended in limbo between the foliage of trees and the meadow below.

By bringing to light the character of the island, Les Jardiniers Nomades encourage visitors to question the future. If the success of the cultural festival contributs largely to educating and connecting visitors to this important heritage area, the question still remains: what history can be written on this 'blank page'?

Top: The cabin of the island becomes a window open to the landscape
Bottom: A panorama on the landscape
Opposite top: A hammock resting area

Top: A terrace overlooking the landscape
Bottom: Moment of reflexion at the heart of the Hortillonnages

Top: A big, inclined hammock

A White Horizon Drawn by Whitewashed Trunks

A White Horizon Drawn by Whitewashed Trunks

Top: A place to enjoy the water
Bottom: Individual hammocks
Opposite top: An alignment of whitewashed trunks pointing out the limits of the island
Opposite bottom: The verticality of whitewashed trunks

12
LE SYNDROME
DE LA PAGE
BLANCHE
Collectif
les jardiniers nomades
H

Wijkeroog Park

Location: Velsen, Netherlands
Area: 47 hectares (116 acres)
Landscape Design: Bureau B+B, Erick de Lyon
Photography: Bureau B+B
Client: Gemeente Velsen

In collaboration with artist Erick de Lyon, Bureau B+B was commissioned to transform Wijkeroog Park in Velsen, Netherlands. By removing the existing fragmentation of spaces and restoring the natural water system in the area, the park has been given a more cohesive recreational and ecological structure.

The lower course of the former Scheybeeck stream guided the reintroduction of the park's watercourse, and has subsequently served as a link for green areas and a guide for a recreational bicycle path. An ancient stream, the Scheybeeck had disappeared over the years and was no longer identifiable as a watercourse. The stream was once fed by fresh water from the landscape but was also subject to the ebbs and flows of the tides. Bureau B+B wanted to restore the lower course of the Scheybeeck and make it visible again in the Wijkeroog Park, but have it follow a new course—one that would give it a new identity and make it an autonomous element within the park.

The stream's new course runs down the park at a natural incline and sits 12 inches (30 centimeters) above ground level. The contrast between the creation of this artificial stream and the new naturalistic and recreational opportunities it presents was a significant element of the design brief. Spatial and connectivity issues were addressed by the new configuration of the Scheybeeck, and the composition

of the park consists of open spaces that alternate with 40-year-old woodland areas. It is in these spaces that the new stream course was staged, producing an interplay for visitors as it vanishes and reappears from view along the length of the park's newly-implemented pedestrian and cycle routes. The positioning of the stream and paths makes full use of sightlines within the park, emphasizing the striking industrial features close by and presenting a constantly changing perspective of the area's green spaces and industrial heritage.

Adapting to the topography of the park, the stream's profile consists of a natural bank roughly 10 to 15 feet (3 to 5 meters) in width. A bespoke concrete element stops drainage of stream water into the groundwater, and also stops it from drying up in summer. Occasionally, the specially-designed bank will overflow, so a rough layer of concrete secures sediment and provides a habitat for microorganisms, and water-resistant clay keeps the bank marshy, allowing for a continuous connection of flora and fauna. Metal bridges that cross the stream are sourced from a nearby steelworks, and their rusty appearance contrasts well with the natural bank.

Observation points allow glimpses into stream life, and are marked by low and narrow crossing points. 'Natural' variation is created in-part by human interference, and elements of play and education are formed by the design of the stream—for example, loose boulders allow children to challenge the flow of the watercourse. Wider areas allow for fishing, wading, and planting alongside the primary function of water storage.

Where the stream enters the North Sea canal, an interesting mix of fresh and brackish water can be observed. Here, an intermediary zone has been designed behind a sea dike, allowing a ribbon of fresh water to flow across the brackish water. This continuous supply of fresh water, combined with the overflow of the brackish water, produces gradients of salinity along the stream's course. In addition, a siphon allows fish and salt water to access the park. Consequently, an interesting mix of habitats is created for flora and fauna. The discharge zone to the North Sea has a salinity gradient of 2000 to 5000 milligrams of chloride per liter, allowing salt water plants such as sea aster and saltmarsh rush to thrive alongside fish like the thicklip grey mullet, sea lamprey, and black goby. This mix of flora and fauna has also given emergence to a foraging area for local birdlife, including the common tern and common merganser.

Top: A pool at the end of an artificial stream
Opposite top: Encounter of a path and stream

Elevation Plan

1. Existing ground level
2. Natural shore
3. Stream profile
4. Existing ground leve land plantings with planting stock
5. Bike lane asphalt in two layers of rubble foundation
6. Water line

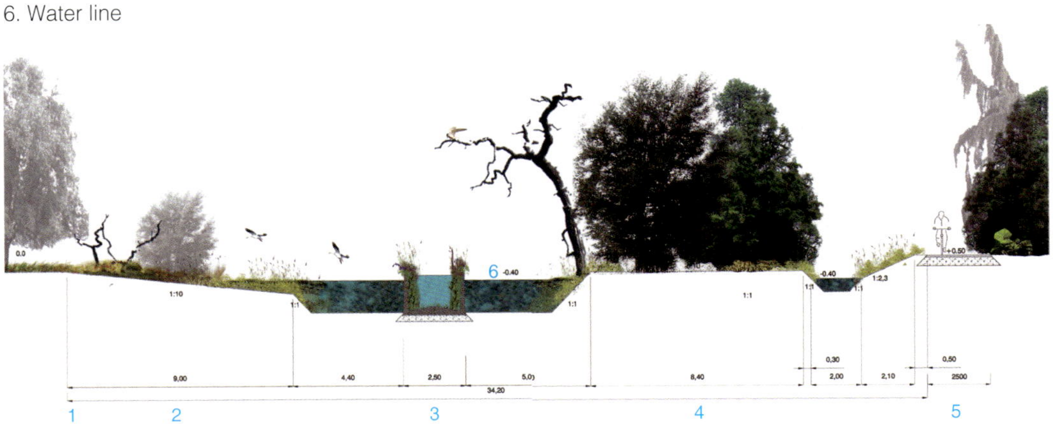

Site Plan

Opposite top: A mix of fresh and brackish water
Opposite bottom left and right: New ecologies

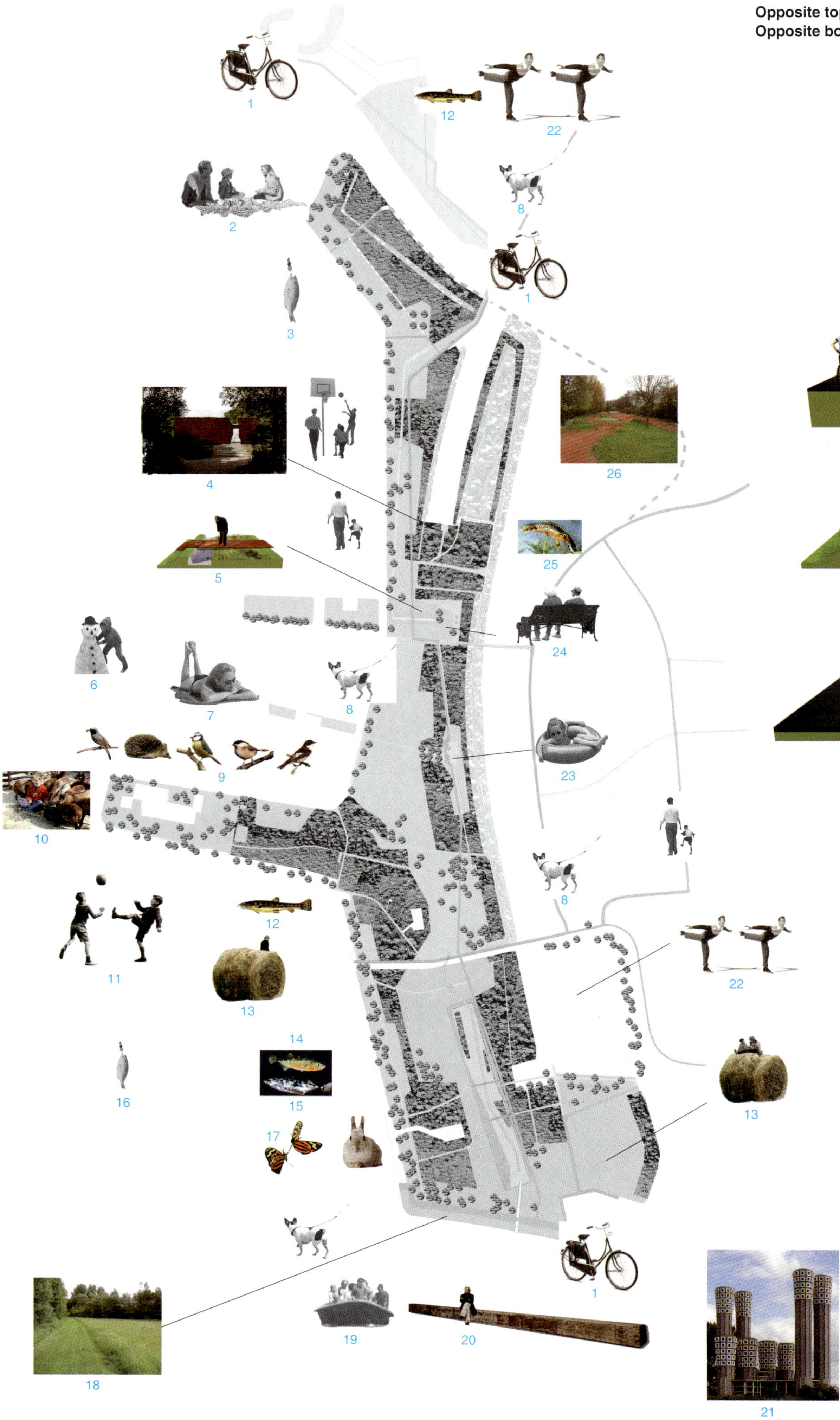

Park Attractions and Activities

1. Biking
2. Picnic area
3. Fishpond
4. Hedge around folly
5. Bridge/observation post
6. Making a snowman
7. Sunbathing
8. Dog walkers
9. Fauna in the forest
10. Petting farm
11. Ball games
12. Fauna Scheybeek
13. Hay stacks
14. Brakish water basin
15. Fauna in brakish water
16. Fish
17. Fauna in meadow
18. Meadow
19. Jetty
20. Viewpoint
21. Velser towers
22. Ice skating pond
23. Padding pool
24. Brookgarden with sitting area
25. Fauna Scheybeek
26. BMX-track

Hillarys Boat Harbour

Location: Hillarys, Perth, Australia
Area: 2.1 hectares (5.19 acres)
Landscape Design: Blackwell & Associates
Photography: Rob Frith, Acorn Photo
Client: Western Australia Department of Transport

Blackwell & Associates were engaged in 2003 to undertake master planning for the redevelopment of Hillarys Boat Harbour and, subsequently, in 2005 commenced detailed documentation and contract administration to implement the first of three main upgrades, the last of which was completed in December 2009.

The design for the overall master plan looked at significantly improving the usability of the entire site, with an emphasis on improving the quality of the visitor experience for families and reducing antisocial activity.

This work incorporated improved circulation paths and access ways, thereby providing visitors with a choice of paths and, more importantly, a circular route around the inner harbor.

This was made possible by the construction of a new pedestrian drawbridge by Cox Architects, which was associated with the new Breakwater Hotel at the harbor.

The finished landscape work involved the construction of wide paths and seating areas, numerous shade shelters, picnic facilities, beach showers, an amphitheater for events and floating screens, extensive lighting linking to car parking areas, and the improvement of beach access for all users.

These works were a huge success in terms of encouraging visitation in a location that is somewhat distant from general commercial areas.

Hillarys Boat Harbour celebrated its 20-year anniversary in 2008, and the harbor has since experienced rapid growth and expansion, and become hugely popular not just as a major tourist precinct, but also as a regional marina and social hub for the burgeoning northern suburbs of Perth. The facility has rapidly developed to become the state's busiest recreational harbor, catering for more than 700 vessels, the northern Rottnest Ferry terminal, and over 4 million visitors a year.

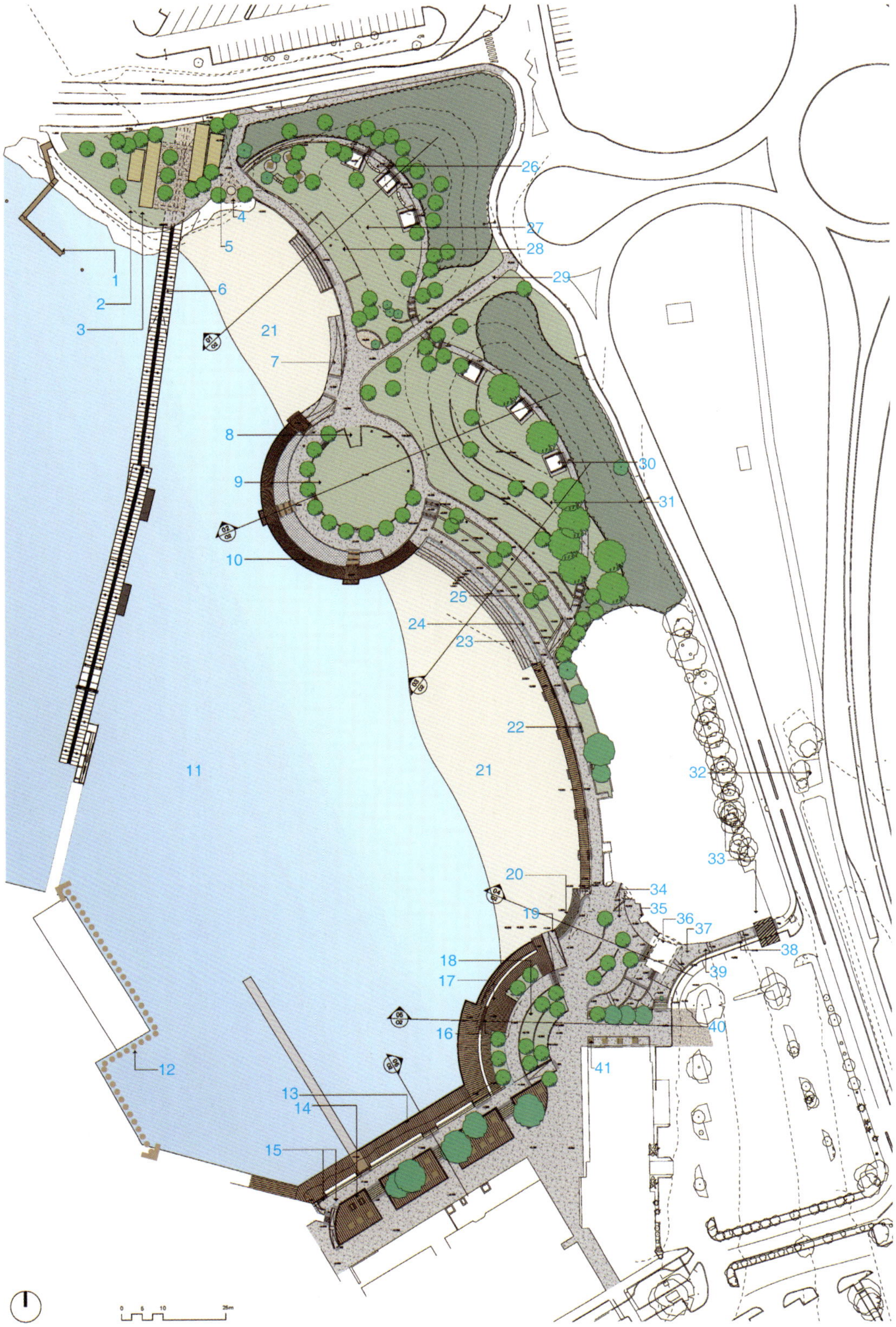

Plan of Stages 1-3 of Hillarys Boat Harbour

1. Possible location for floating pontoon with disabled access
2. Reinforced grassed emergency access
3. Possible future cafe/kiosk locations
4. Rotary 'dolphin wishing well'
5. Arrival and meeting area
6. Link by others
7. Disabled access grade ramp for beach cleaning
8. Maintenance access to lawn
9. Central raised 'event' lawn
10. Center groyne boardwalk with ramped disabled access
11. Harbor
12. Boardwalk connection
13. Proposed timber boardwalk
14. Timber deck stage/seating
15. Wheelchair access ramps
16. Two-level disabled access timber boardwalk
17. Dual purpose shaded area
18. Raised grass seating lawn
19. Ramp for tractor and emergency vehicles
20. Broad steps to beach
21. Beach
22. Access to lawn area
23. Broad steps to beach
24. Path
25. Broad grass terraces
26. Barbecue picnic shelters
27. Informal picnic and boat show area
28. Vehicle access
29. Regraded entry path providing clear views to harbor from roundabout
30. Shade shelters and seating
31. Informal terraces
32. Wheelchair access to bus stop
33. Access into theme park to be adjusted
34. Paved 'beach' with universal access
35. Access to toilets
36. Proposed building
37. Access ramp
38. Proposed retaining wall
39. Increased width to main access path adjacent to parallel parking
40. Main entrance to harbor precinct
41. Fixed bench table settings

Opposite top: Screening of the picnic lawns
Opposite bottom: Beach and picnic lawn

Top: Artwork and picnic lawn
Bottom: Center groyne protection and beach ramp
Opposite top: Picnic shelters
Opposite bottom: Beach walk and lawn area

PLEASE RESPECT THE LAW
ALCOHOL FREE VENUE

Elizabeth Hills Estate, Hoxton Park

Location: Hoxton Park, Sydney, Australia
Area: 15.25 hectares (37.68 acres)
Landscape Design: Sturt Noble Associates
Photography: Sturt Noble Associates
Client: Mirvac/Urban Growth NSW

Mirvac and Urban Growth NSW engaged Sturt Noble Associates to create a master plan and design all landscape elements for this planned residential estate in outer suburban Sydney. The master plan provides for large areas of open space linked to form a system of parks with connections to the Western Sydney Parklands, an already established urban park system.

The design team developed the entire estate entry experience, including the main entry bridge, streetscapes, and an open space corridor encompassing a cycle path and timber boardwalks. Scope included the major parkland, Hill Top Park, which includes a playground, barbecue area, shelters, and public art.

Elizabeth Hills displays pioneering techniques in implementing Water Sensitive Urban Design (WSUD), creating a naturalistic habitat system to enhance biodiversity and ecosystems in the area. The site encompasses 139 acres (56.27 hectares), of which 30 acres (12.14 hectares) is riparian corridor land.

The challenge was to create and implement innovative methods of water management, incorporating landscaping, engineering, and ecological design in the treatment of the tributaries of nearby Hinchinbrook Creek. The design solution implemented a total catchment concept for the riparian corridor with WSUD features

Top: Covered picnic and barbeque area in Hill Top Park
Opposite top: Pergolas provide shaded seating adjacent to the play area

located in the core riparian zone, while simultaneously meeting ecological targets.

Best practice environmental design techniques have been integrated in the development. This includes wetland design, riparian rehabilitation, creekline reconstruction, bioengineering, bush regeneration, and protection of threatened Cumberland Plain Woodland areas (the name for a distinct grouping of plants that occur on the clay soils derived from shale on the undulating Cumberland Plain in central New South Wales), which Hinchinbrook Creek is part of.

Careful planning was carried out to ensure minimal disruption to all significant trees on the site. Seed collection and sourcing of indigenous species was coordinated, with all plants for the area contract grown on site.

Sturt Noble Associates also designed bioengineering works and channel batters for a relocated creek channel. This included specification of rockwork, soil logs, and recycling felled trees in order to achieve soil stablization and habitat creation.

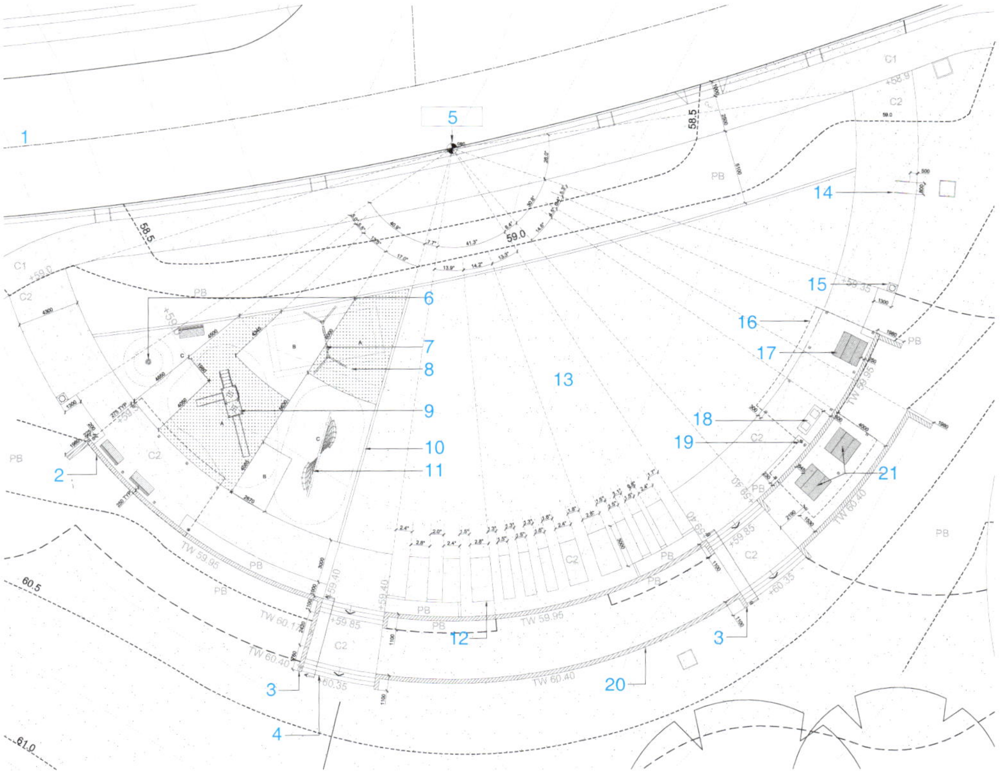

Construction Issue A1

1. Road
2. Pergola
3. Wall
4. Concrete steps
5. Set out point for radius
6. Twista
7. Double swing
8. Rubber softfall
9. Slide
10. Concrete edge
11. Hemisphere climber
12. Paving
13. Lawn area
14. Bike rack
15. Bin
16. Pergola
17. Table and bench
18. Barbecue area
19. Tap and drain
20. Retaining wall
21. Furniture

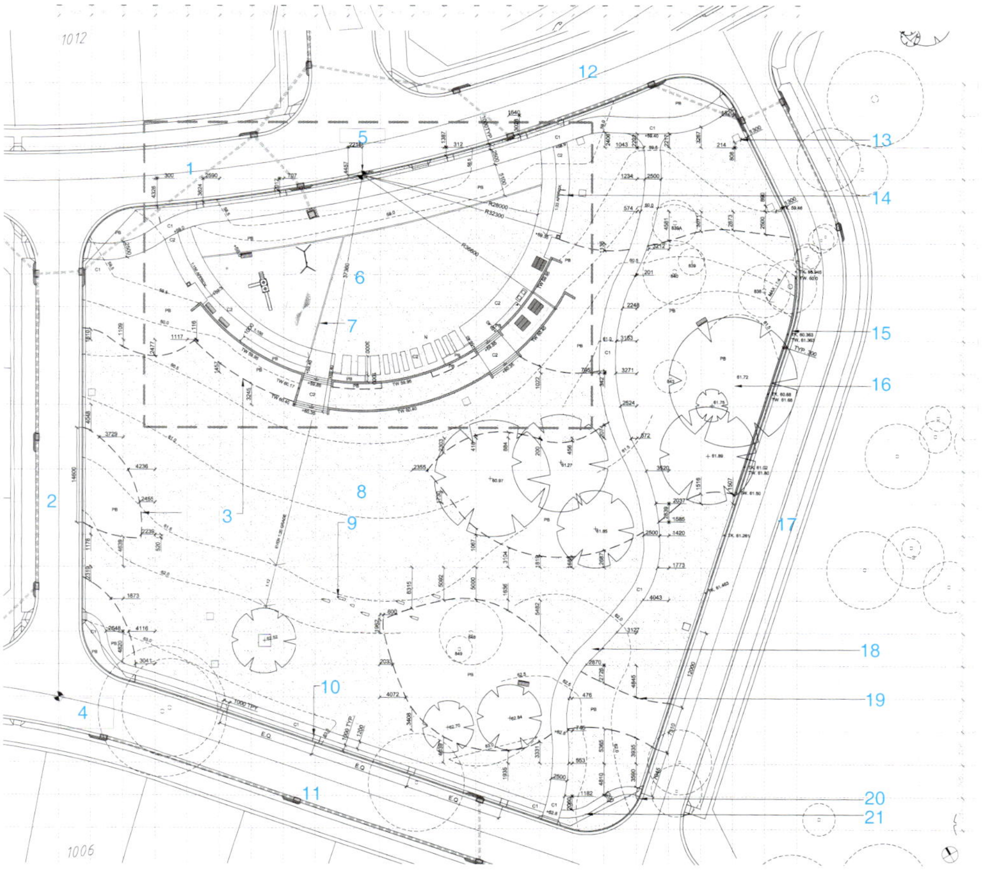

CD-1009-03 REV E A1

1. Road
2. Road
3. Garden Eedging
4. Set out point for 5m grid based on road
5. Set out point for radius
6. Amphitheater
7. Concrete edging
8. Lawn area
9. Sculptures
10. Timber edging
11. Road
12. Road
13. Tree pit
14. Bicycle rack
15. Retaining wall to align with park boundary
16. Existing trees to be retained and protected
17. Road
18. Concrete shared path
19. Garden edging
20. Pram ramp
21. Concrete pedestrian footpath

Top: Timber boardwalks provide access to the creek
Bottom: Road bridge is reflected in the tranquil waters of the creek
Opposite top: Viewing areas are located along the creekline

Top: A shared pathway crosses the creek, providing access for residents
Bottom: Plants and rocks provide protection against flooding
Opposite top: Playground
Opposite bottom: Artwork highlights the agricultural heritage of the area

Rivermouth Park

Location: Schwäbisch Gmünd, Germany
Area: 15 hectares (37 acres)
Landscape Design: A24 Landschaft Landschaftsarchitektur GmbH
Photography: Hanns Joosten
Client: Landesgartenschau Schwäbisch Gmünd 2014 GmbH

Schwäbisch Gmünd, a town in southern Germany, has engineered a far-reaching urban redevelopment process, resulting in a new green heart for the city. This comprehensive project has structurally reoriented the inner city, including its traffic patterns. As part of the redevelopment, historical urban structures were exposed, new urban axes were formed, and expansive public spaces were built. A new image of the inner city has been forged by a boulevard, a green promenade, paths, and public squares along the old urban streams, as well as sporting areas and playgrounds. A24's responsibilities ranged from planning the overall urban development concept down to designing the individual details.

A symbol for this new Gmünd is the reclamation of a central open area: the long overbuilt outlet of the Josefsbach—a small brook—into the Rems—a larger stream. This river mouth (Mündung in German) is the source of the city's name.

The water junction has become a link between the new and existing open areas in Gmünd. Located between the train station and the old town, it links the old baroque city garden, the Remspark, open spaces along the Josefsbach, and the passages to the old town, which converge to form a new, spacious green zone. Each of these areas opens onto the river, imbuing it with a rich play of various relationships to, and perspectives on, the water.

Top: The new green promenade corridor provides space for a water feature

This new city center was made possible by the construction of a traffic tunnel and the spatial reorientation that accompanied it, which included the removal and relocation of streets, the demolition of buildings, and the creation and accentuation of new urban development axes. Critical prerequisites for the accessibility and redevelopment of the water area were the raising of the riverbed up to 13 feet (4 meters) and the flattening of the formerly steep riverbanks.

Where the nearby highway once carried 35,000 vehicles daily along four lanes, today it has given way to a leafy boulevard lined with ginkgo trees, creating a new entrance to Schwäbisch Gmünd.

The new urban development axes lead from the train station forecourt, over the junction of the Rems and Josefsbach, through the reopened Ledergasse (German for 'leather alley') and into the historic center of the city.

Ledergasse traverses the entire length of the Josenvorstadt, which arose in the 14th century as part of an early expansion of the city. Originally settled by tanners, the street became one of Gmünd's main shopping streets in 1977 upon the construction of a major department store, whose massive structure disrupted the formerly intact thoroughfare and cut it off from the junction of the Josefsbach and the Rems. Over the course of the city's current urban development transformation, the area around the department store was reorganized and the building demolished, such that Ledergasse now opens onto the river and the former backstreet has become vibrant once again. The redesign incorporates historical elements: the former watercourse through the 'Bächle' arch in

Top: The old baroque city garden was carefully transformed

Ledergasse is referenced as a shallow stream in the natural stone paving. As a result—and with the addition of seating along the street—Ledergasse has become a popular place to linger.

The new Josefsbach Promenade begins at the river mouth and creates a green ring as it encircles the old town. By the water it becomes a sculpted riverway, narrowing and widening to create a variety of perspectives and spatial effects. The part of the promenade at street level, above the restored historic city wall, connects the old town to the river through a series of public squares and playgrounds.

Within the immediate vicinity of the city center, spacious open areas were developed for cross-generational sporting activities. The new activities strip runs alongside the new promenade, as well as over the railway tracks to the Gleispark youth recreation area. One particular highlight is the Netzvilla, a climbing frame resembling a multistory villa. As tall as a house, the enclosed apparatus forms a complex three-dimensional structure, creating a play space almost 26 feet (8 meters) high.

The comprehensive spatial revaluation and urban development of the inner city—which had formerly suffered from a lack of green areas—along with the attractive open spaces along the water and the broad spectrum of recreational offerings strengthens the urban core, provides healthy competition for surrounding communities, and sustainably gears this traditional town for the future.

Top: The city center was completely transformed, with the removal of streets and the demolition of buildings
Opposite top: The new Josefsbach Promenade creates a green ring as it encircles the old town
Opposite bottom: The promenade incorporates the long-forgotten urban stream into the city and creates an attractive new open area

Top: The riverside path runs alongside the city's medieval defence wall and crosses a series of historic bridges
Bottom: The historic structures were restored and delicately expanded through contemporary design
Opposite top: Playgrounds, sport facilities, and cross-generational activities round out the redevelopment
Opposite bottom left: Climbing sculpture with colored wooden elements
Opposite bottom right: The Netzvilla: a climbing frame as tall as a house that forms a complex three-dimensional structure

Park in Casalmoro

Location: Casalmoro, Lombardy, Italy
Area: 1 hectare (2.47 acres)
Landscape Design: Archiplanstudio
Photography: Martina Mambrin
Client: Municipality of Casalmoro

The banks of Chiese, a 100 mile (160 kilometer) river that borders Casalmoro in the Italian region of Lombardy, has been a meeting place for many generations over the centuries, however in the past 20 years there has been a move away from activities that take place along the river.

The project plan was to redevelop and promote the area and encourage people to use it once again. 'Chiesenatico' is the name by which past generations defined the afternoons spent on the river Chiese's beaches.

This ironic name (which references Cesenatico, a seaside town on the Adriatic Coast), describes the community's deep relationship with the river, and shows how the riverbank was perceived as a faraway land, full of the charms and dreams often associated with holiday resorts.

As part of the redevelopment the banks of the river were rebuilt, allowing visitors to rediscover the ancient relationship with the river.

Waterways are often seen as hostile and dangerous places, and this perception limits the creation of structures that can bring people closer to the water. To address this, platforms made from wooden panels, natural stone, and Corten steel were built. They were designed

to fit around and enhance the presence of the existing trees, and reinforced steel tubes offer resistance to flood waters.

This small intervention encourages visitors to once again experience the river, and also creates conditions for the creation and development of a new riparian forest.

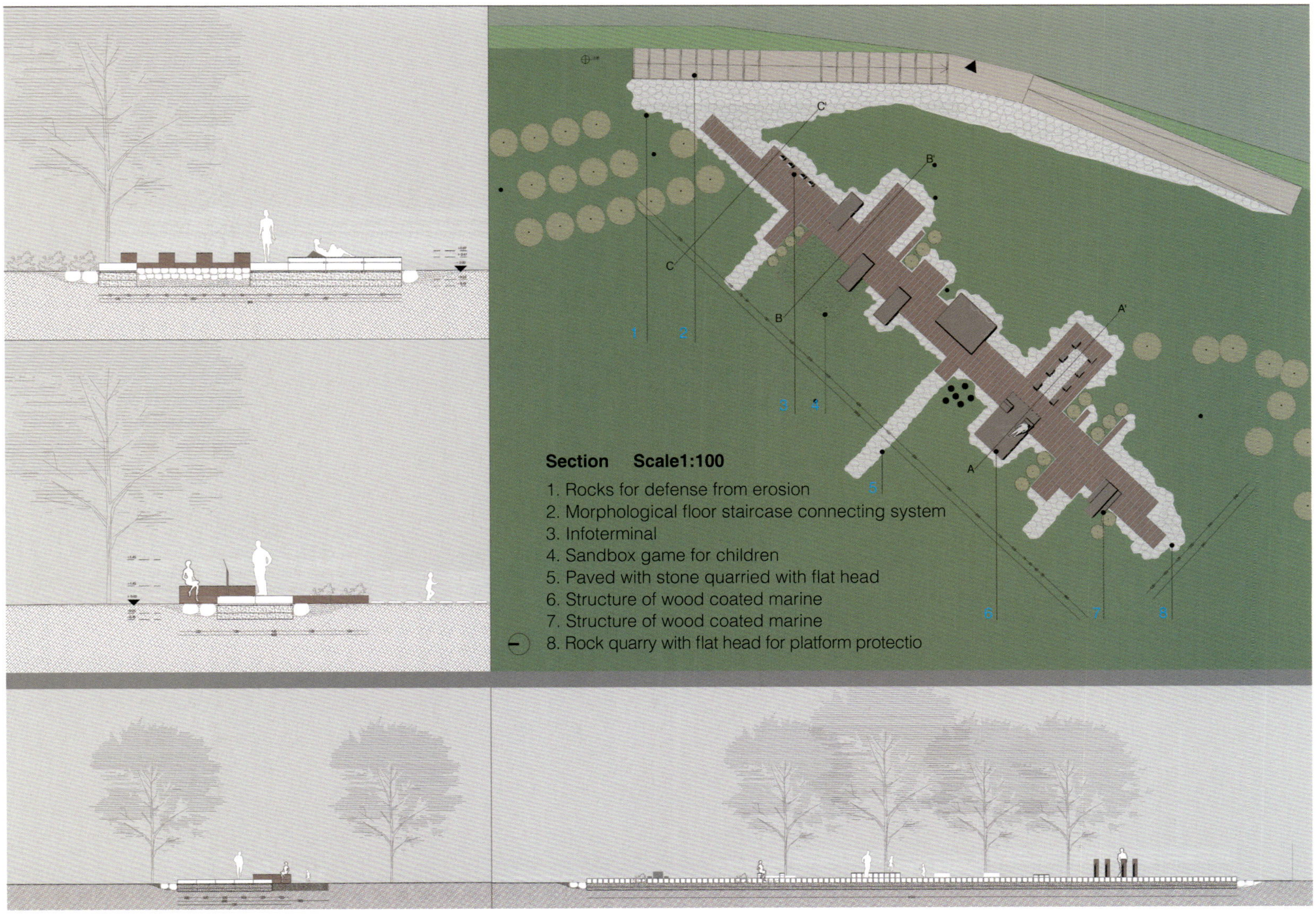

Bottom/Opposite top and bottom: Rest area with information panels

Top: Portion of the seating area in full sun
Bottom: Detail of the seats
Opposite top: Portion of the seating area in the shade
Opposite bottom: Detai of the seats

Marzahn Recreational Park

Location: Marzahn, Berlin, Germany
Area: 4.5 hectares (11.12 acres)
Landscape Design: Rehwaldt Landscape Architects
Photographer: Rehwaldt Landscape Architects
Client: Grüen Berlin Park und Garten GmbH

The Marzahn Recreational Park arose out of the Berlin Garden Show, held in 1987, and presents a collection of garden design from around the world.

It was initially inspired by English landscape gardens, and two examples of this design style are the park's curved paths and large meadows.

Over the past few decades, tree groups have formed distinctive characteristic spaces, and the gentle topography of the Wuhle Valley has been integrated into the open space concept, with the Kienberg Mountain forming a backdrop to the park.

Rehwaldt were engaged to redevelop the park, with the idea of maintaining the park's existing character while establishing new attractions, such as thematic playgrounds, and promoting environmental education.

As part of the expansion, it was possible to offer quiet recreational sites and new attractions for visitors. While most new areas have been planned as large meadows, the area at Blumberger Damm is infrastructural in nature, with car parking, access, and logistics catering for greater numbers of visitors. A new visitor center and restaurant will also be implemented nearby.

New walking paths take visitors through meadows and around existing tree groups. As part of the first stage of development, existing willow trees and populous plants were spatially rearranged, and subsequent plantings (e.g. oaks, maples, chestnuts) complement these tree groups.

The relationship between the original English layout and its German interpretation is significant. The English-style layout was used as spatial frame in which the different cultural gardens were integrated. By expanding the gardens of the world to the south green, these spaces have been redeveloped.

The mesic area at Marzahn-Hellersdorf Brook, a small tributary valley of the Wuhle, were maintained and integrated into the park. In this way, diversified fragmented gardens set within a spacious landscape create interspatial tension. This situation was accentuated by the addition a few design elements, such as a boardwalk leading over the marsh area, allowing visitors to experience various flora and fauna.

Through realignment of the area, it was possible for the first time since opening in 1987 to plan a new entrance to the park. This new entrance was aimed at integrating the gardens of the world concept with the urban neighborhood in which the park sits. A wooden deck was built, offering vast views across the park, and the terrace and adjacent area can also be used for hosting different events.

Top: Panorama of Marzahn Recreational Park
Bottom: A path made of bricks and wood
Opposite top: Path surrounded by green vegetation

Concept Plan

Top left and right: Brick paths in the park
Bottom right: Renderings of one part of the park
Opposite top: Lush plants in the park

Clifton Hill Railway Park

Location: Clifton Hill, Victoria, Australia
Area: 1.2 hectares (2.97 acres)
Landscape Design: Jeavons Landscape Architects
Photography: Andrew Lloyd Photography
Client: Victoria Department of Transport

The duplication of the railway track between Clifton Hill and Westgarth Stations was a key initiative to improve Melbourne's public transport service, and required a second rail bridge to be constructed over Merri Creek.

Jeavons Landscape Architects were responsible for implementing a complex landscape architectural brief and the design of green infrastructure along the new track and in the adjoining Merri Creek corridor. The project required the blending of technically challenging design with aesthetics and high community expectations.

Based on scientific research by the Australian Research Centre for Urban Ecology, the design sought to recreate indigenous flora communities of similar species composition and structure to the original ecology.

After rigorous research, a large number of local indigenous plants were installed. The planting has proved to be extremely successful and requires little maintenance.

As a result of Jeavons's advocacy and designs, a new park was also created under the railway bridge. Comprising a series of vegetated terraces defined by dramatic curving walls, and dissected by a recreation spine complete with basketball court, mounded asphalt,

'hang out' rocks, and a raingarden, this space has been well adopted by people in the local community.

This project demonstrates how landscape architecture integrates the professions of planning, architecture, engineering, and specialty technical interests, elevating the restoration of a significant creek landscape, and recognizing the complex interests of diverse local communities.

Top: View of south bank from High Street Bridge. New Merri Creek Trail and ramp access addressing the grades of the site
Bottom: Ecological restoration has been wildly successful. Clematis microphylla scrambles up and over gabions and Corten. Shade trees will improve urban amenity and reduce heat island effect
Opposite top: Panorama showing the new bridge, Merri creek, planting and Merri Trail

South Bank Grading and Hardscape Works

1. High Street
2. Retain and protect existing bridge balustrade
3. Reinstate all signs, footpaths, and kerbs to High Street to match existing, retain existing bluestone monument
4. Bike BL
5. Rail fence
6. Path
7. Raised bluestone kerb edge

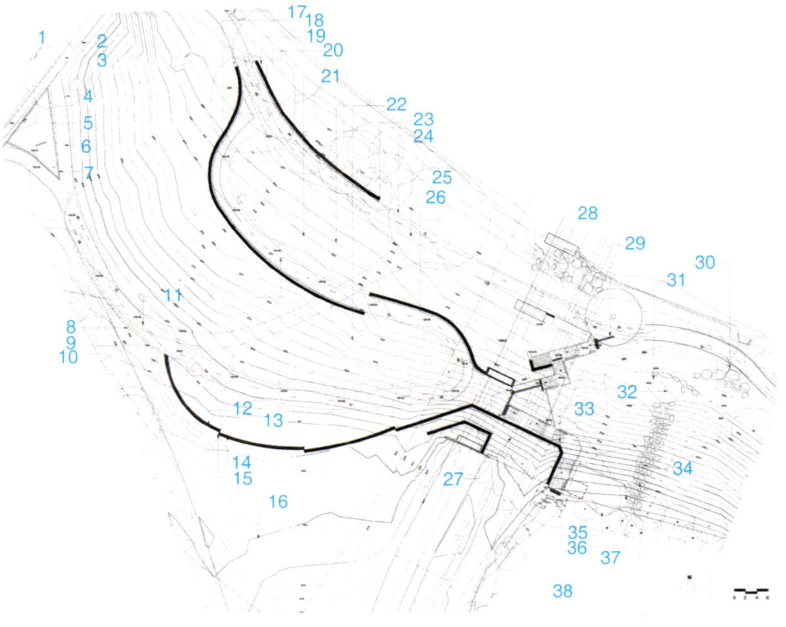

8. Rail fence
9. Vehicle gates
10. Ramp for vehicle access
11. Path
12. Rail fence
13. Excavate existing to create terrace beside new gabion wall
14. Gabion retaining wall
15. Crushed concrete surfacing to railway yard
16. Railway yard
17. Grade in new path to meet up with existing path levels
18. Gabion walls
19. Gabion wall to retain merri creek trail
20. Bike HR
21. Regrade slope establish channel and ridge line beside path
22. Regrade existing slope to accommodate new path
23. Ensure ends of handrail are min 1m from side of path
24. Reinstate merri creek trail to new levels,path to be red concrete with exposed aggregate to match existing merri creek trail standard treatment
25. Concrete edge
26. Bike BL
27. Bluestone cladding to embankment
28. Merri Creek
29. Path
30. Engineers to design and construct overflow/headwall. Overflow water to flow below path in existing drainage outlet to creek
31. Garde new wetland into base of slope
32. Centre line through wetland
33. Staircase and lookout
34. Drainage channels
35. Lookout area
36. Stormwater outlet
37. Design and construct litter trap to main drain
38. Coulson Reserve

Legend

- Riparian planting
- Escarpment planting
- Grassy woodland planting
- Merri Creek
- Proposed pedestrian/cycle link
- Proposed trees
- Existing vegetation
- Proposed pedestrian/cycle link
- Maintenance and pedestrian access path
- Existing bridge piers
- New bridge piers

Landscape Concept Design

1. Urquhart Street
2. High Street
3. Merri Creek
4. Creek Parade
5. Creek valley landscape
6. Railway yard
7. Coulson Reserve
8. Embankments
9. Vacant rail land
10. Investigate remodelling creek
11. Pedestrain and cycle access
12. Path link to Clifton Hill Station

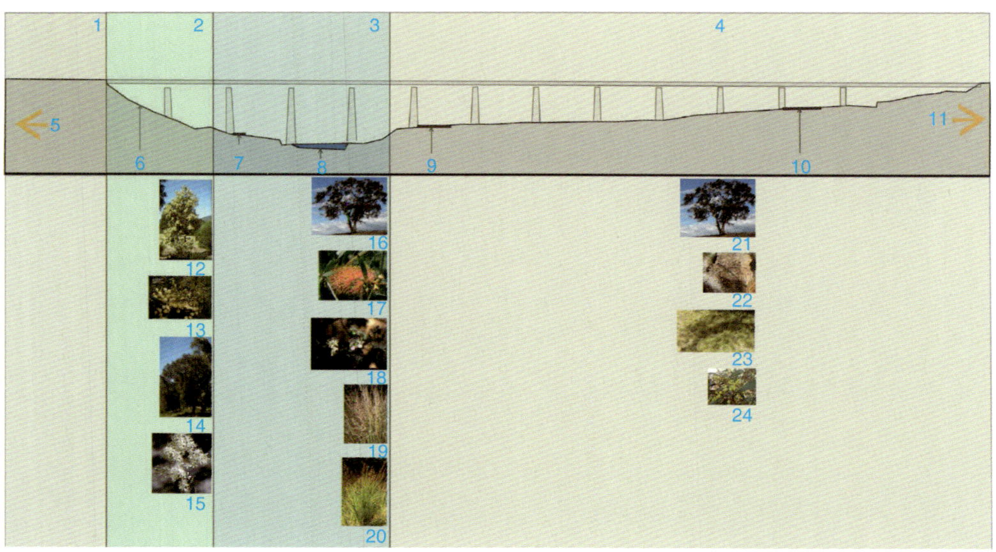

Vegetation Classes and Key Species

1. Grassy woodland
2. Escarpment shrubland
3. Riparian scrub, riparian woodland, creekline tussock grassland, stream bank shrubland
4. Grassy woodland
5. To Clifton Hill Station and Coulson Reserve
6. Proposed capital city trail
7. Existing capital city trail
8. Merri Creek
9. Creek parade
10. Urquhart Street
11. To Westgarth Station
12. Acacia implexa
13. Acacia mearnsii
14. Allocasuarina verticillata
15. Bursaria spinosa
16. Eucalyptus camaldulensis
17. Callistemon sieberi
18. Leptospermum lanigerum
19. Poa labillardieri
20. Carex appressa
21. Eucalyptus camaldulensis
22. Themeda triandra
23. Austrodanthonia
24. Acacia pycnantha

Top: Grassy woodland planting frames Bridge Park. Basketball hoops have been installed below the bridge. In the far distance, stairs and native plants can be seen on the south bank

Elevation A: Merri Creek Embankment

1. Predominantly low plantings for visiblity from new path system
2. Clifton Hill Junction
3. New path configuration linking High Street to the Merri Creek Trail, and Merri Creek Trail to Coulson Reserve; the escarpment planting is predominantly local provenance and native species
4. Merri Creek Trail
5. Merri Creek Embankment and ephemeral planting

Elevation B: Bridge Park

1. Westgarth Station
2. Westgarth Street
3. Cunningham Street
4. Walker Street
5. Hurstbridge Railway Line
6. Urquhart Street
7. To Rushall Station
8. Merri Creek
9. High Street
10. To Clifton Hill Station
11. Garden bed with predomonantly local provenance and native planting
12. Ephermeral wetland with local tuft and sedge planting
13. Hard surface play area with basketball court and play line markings under the railway lines
14. Predomonantly local provenance grass planted among recycled railway sleepers

South Bank Grading and Hardscape Works

1. Carefully remove existing bluestone and reuse for new kerb alignment
2. New bluestone kerb alignment to match existing
3. Modify and reinstate speed hump to match existing paved surface as required
4. New bluestone kerb alignment to match existing
5. Retain and protect existing powerpole and light
6. All asphalt areas to have flush concrete edge
7. Asphalt mound
8. Concrete retaining wall
9. New inground sleepers and railway track
10. Concrete retaining wall
11. Basketball court
12. Concret ramp
13. Concrete pavement with painted ball play lines
14. Basketball ring
15. Concrete retaining wall
16. Cladding to pier
17. Concrete path
18. Colored concrete pavement
19. Concrete retaining wall
20. Boulder field of basalt floaters
21. Recycled crushed brike surfacing
22. Remove existing timber barriers
23. Concrete edge
24. Basalt floaters in concrete
25. Concrete seat wall
26. Creek bank protection
27. Urquhart Street
28. Creek Parade
29. Carefully remove existing bluestone and reuse for new kerb alignment
30. New entry pier
31. Bolt down bench seat product:metro
32. Concrete steps paved and faced with sawn bluestone and charcoal colored mortar
33. Asphalt mound
34. Concrete retaining wall
35. Grade asphalt pavement
36. Railway track fixed to sleepers
37. Concrete retaining seat walls
38. Concrete seat wall
39. Concrete retaining wall
40. Fire break access
41. Timber fence
42. Concrete retaining wall
43. Pebble lined swale drain
44. Removable, recycled plastic bollards
45. Timber crossing
46. Service vehicle access
47. Concrete wall
48. Crushed brick-zone for future artworks

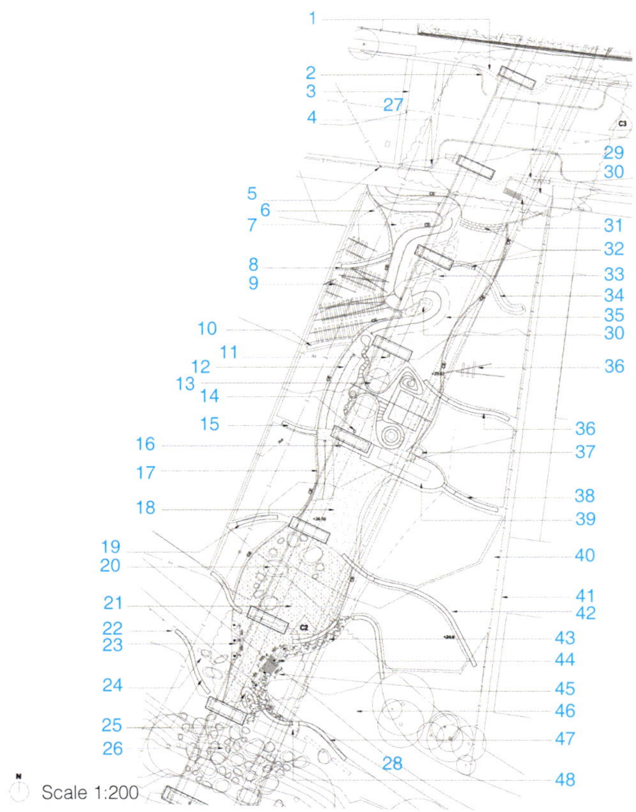

Top: The railway crossing was modified to ensure safety and allow for wheelchair access
Bottom left: Skaters at Bridge Park-Undulating pavement and low walls create unusual street skating spaces. Disabled and maintenance access carefully designed into the sculpted pavement between the piers
Bottom right: Indigenous grasses have been planted around recycled railway tracks, providing an industrial aesthetic
Opposite top: Pavement gradients were carefully calculated, seamlessly integrating access from High Street, Merri Creek Trail and Clifton Hill

Edinburgh Gardens Raingarden

Location: Melbourne, Australia
Area: 700 square meters (7535 square feet)
Landscape Design: GHD
Photography: GHD
Client: Melbourne Water in collaboration with the City of Yarra

The Edinburgh Gardens Raingarden is an initiative that addresses two longstanding environmental problems on the site: polluted stormwater going from drains into local creeks and rivers, and the use of and dependence on drinking water to irrigate significant trees in the gardens.

The form of the raingarden was strongly driven by function and a desire to construct a contemporary structure that would be a counterpoint to the heritage features of this historic park.

The raingarden captures and cleans stormwater before discharging it into storage. The stormwater treatment function dictated the size and the necessity of terracing for optimal water treatment. The junction of the terraces also became an opportunity to bring sections of nearby lawn into the raingarden.

The raingarden recedes into the landscape and doesn't obstruct the long lawn views that characterize the park, and is barely visible from most areas. Sunken lower than the surrounding lawns, the design ensures there are no fall heights of more than 3 feet (1 meter) that would require a visually obstructive balustrade.

The publicly-accessible raingarden elements are constructed in materials like steel and concrete, which are durable, resist damage,

and cope with continual submersion in water. Although robust, the materials are of a high quality and finish.

The most significant element of the raingarden is its ability to provide good environmental outcomes while respecting the park's cultural heritage and traditional uses.

It is designed to remove suspended solids, nutrients, phosphorous, and nitrogen that would otherwise end up in Melbourne's waterways.

Filtered water is used to irrigate existing trees and sports ovals within Edinburgh Gardens, providing around 60 percent of its irrigation needs in a normal year.

The raingarden has been embraced by the local community for the benefits it provides to the park's shady avenues, the improvements to stormwater quality, and the improved health of the local ecosystem.

Top: Southeastern view of the raingarden
Opposite top: The raingarden runs parallel to a shared path

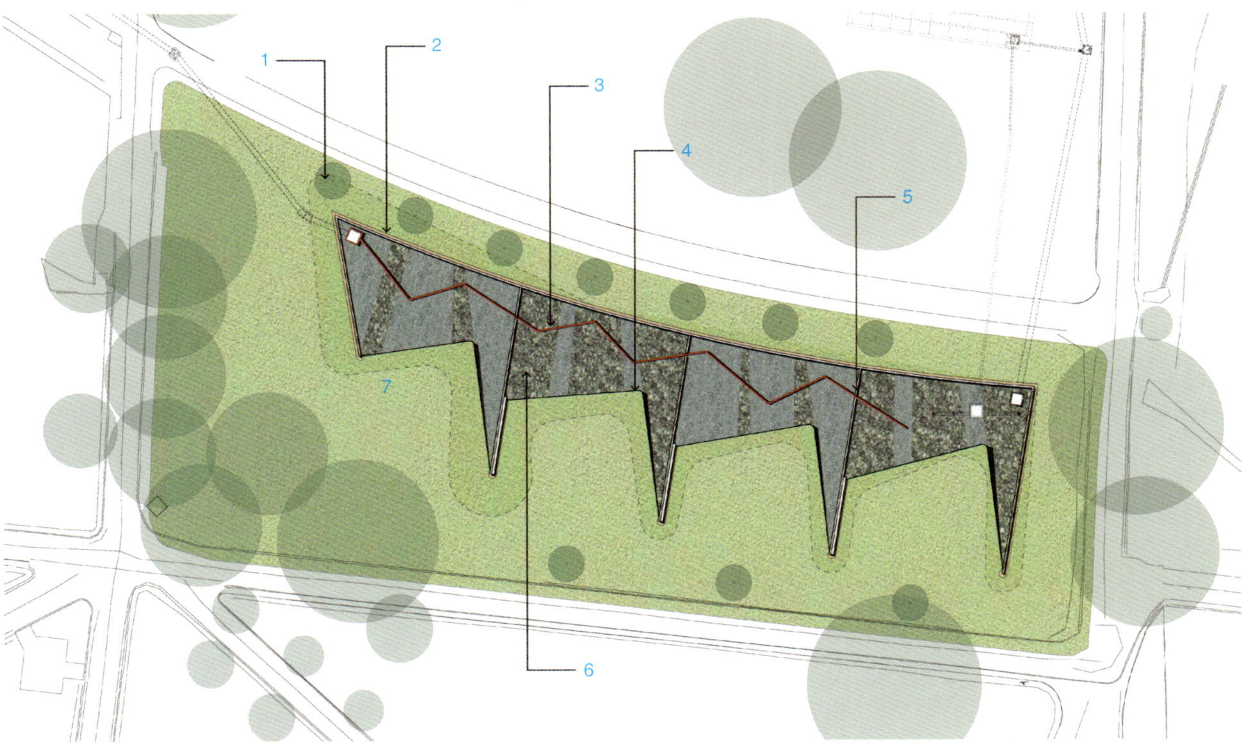

Raingarden Plan

1. New avenue planting
2. Concrete wall
3. Low flow channel
4. Steel edging
5. Concrete terrace wall
6. Bands of planting
7. Raised lawns

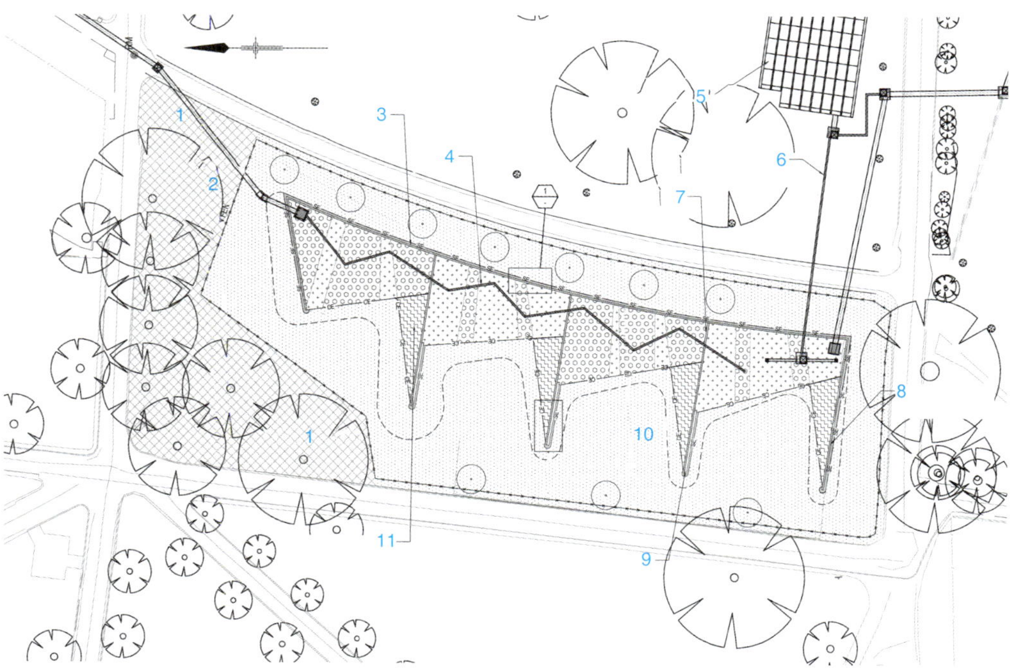

General Arrangement Plan **Scale 1:25**

1. Tree protection zone
2. Tree protection fence
3. Wall
4. Low flow channel
5. Underground water storage
6. Pipe connection from raingarden to storage
7. Wall
8. Wall
9. Wall
10. Top of batter
11. Mulch of garden beds to match aggregate size of Adjacent rain garden

Top: The low flow channel distributes water to the terraces
Opposite top: Lawn 'fingers' extend into the garden

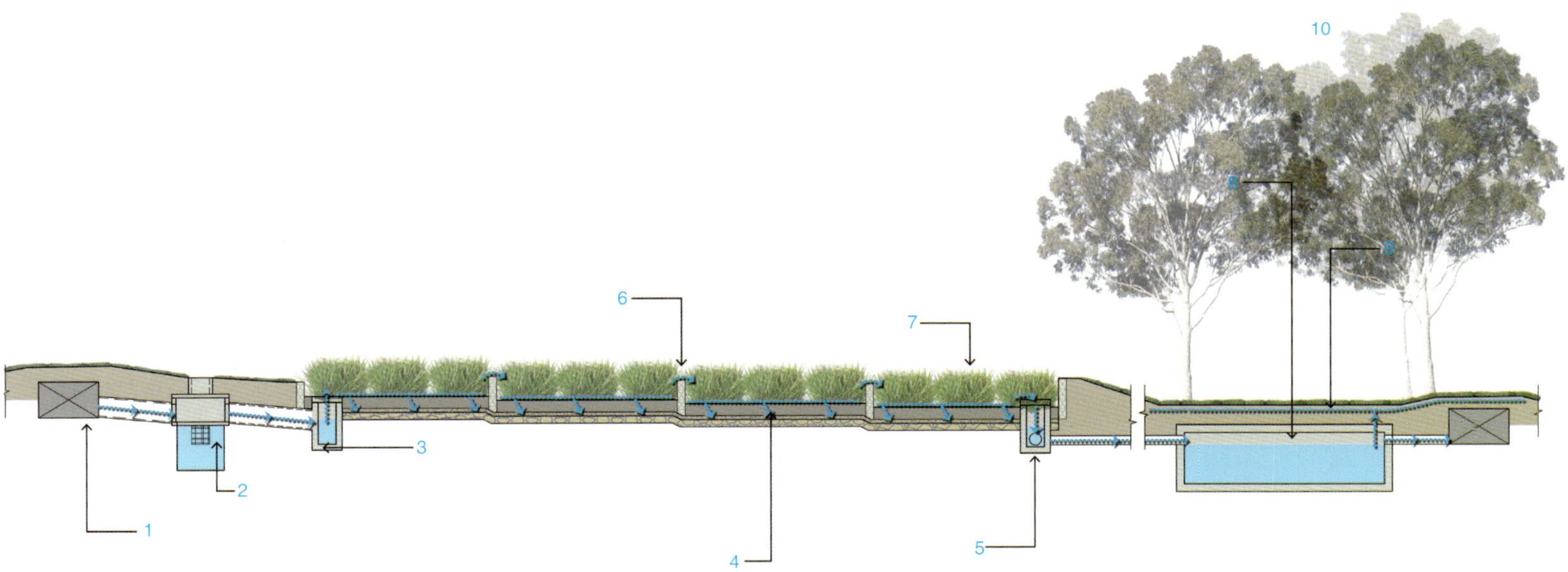

A Schematic Section of the Raingarden

1. North Fitzroy main drain
2. Gross pollutant trap
3. Inlet surcharge pit
4. Water filtered through raingarden
5. Outlet pit to storage
6. Terraced raingarden to naturally clean stormwater
7. Native plants
8. Underground storage
9. Subsurface irrigation of trees in park
10. Existing trees

Top: The curve of the raingarden follows the existing shared trail link through the park
Bottom: View of top portion of the raingarden, looking northeast
Opposite top and bottom: The low flow channel in the Edinburgh Gardens Raingarden

Strubben Kniphorstbosch

Location: Anloo, Netherlands
Area: 295 hectares (728.96 acres)
Landscape Design: Strootman Landschapsarchitecten
Photography: Strootman Landschapsarchitecten
Client: Dutch Forestry Commission

Strubben Kniphorstbos, a woodland and heathland in the catchment area of the Drentsche Aa River, is by far the largest archaeological monument in the Netherlands. As a result of continuous settlement over more than 5000 years, the area abounds in archaeological, historico-geographical, and historico-ecological features.

Until recently the area had been managed as a nature reserve and military training ground, which saved it from agricultural reclamation, and explains why the layout was rugged with large areas of forest. The land passed into the hands of the Dutch Forestry Commission, who decided to work on a development and maintenance plan, with the aim of combining nature conservation and the protection of a heritage area in a contemporary architectural design.

A unique feature of the area is the strubben—strangely shaped oak trees that grew when the area was still a heath and was intensively grazed by sheep. The sheep stripped the young oaks of their leaves, resulting in what now most resembles bonsai. Despite this, some of the oaks managed to develop into mature trees. With the drop in intensity of grazing on the heath during the 20th century, the old trees were gradually taken over by young, spontaneous growth. One of the measures adopted in the design of the park was to free these old trees from the growth so they could be admired once again in all their glory. These interventions will also bring about extremely

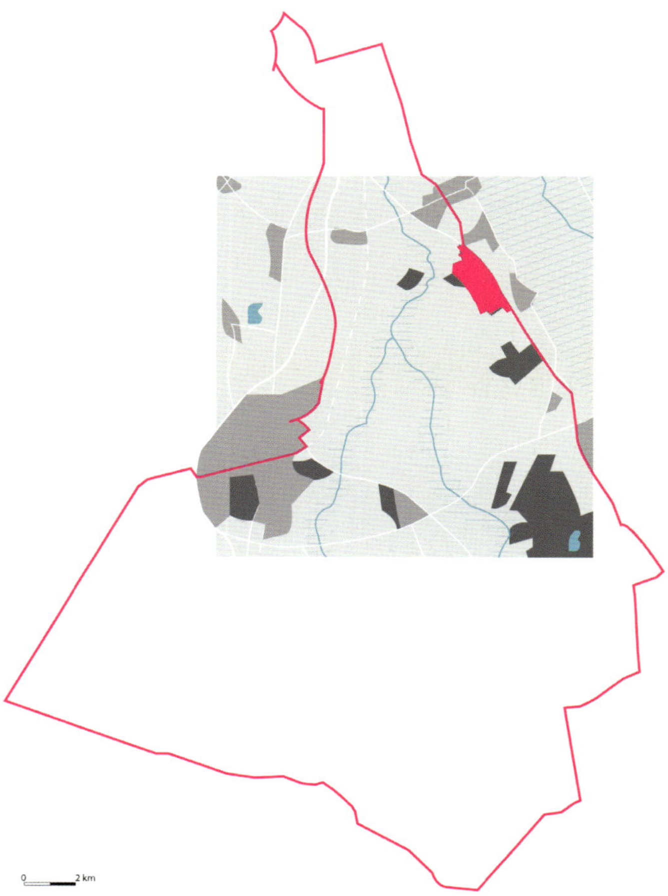

rich ecological gradients of the varied landscape. Furthermore, rare species will be given plenty of new opportunities, and this will also be dramatized by the differences between nature and cultivation. Grazing sheep will also ensure that the open sections of the planning area remain that way.

The resulting development and management plan for the land focuses on the local scenery. The design enhances the contrast between the non-reclaimed landscape and the rationally organized reclamation landscape in the center of the planning area. The plan seizes opportunities to increase the visibility and spatial coherence between traces from the past, enabling visitors to be impressed by the overwhelming amount of history in the area.

Top: Burial mound
Opposite top: Oak shrubs overgrown by spontaneous vegetation (before execution of the design)

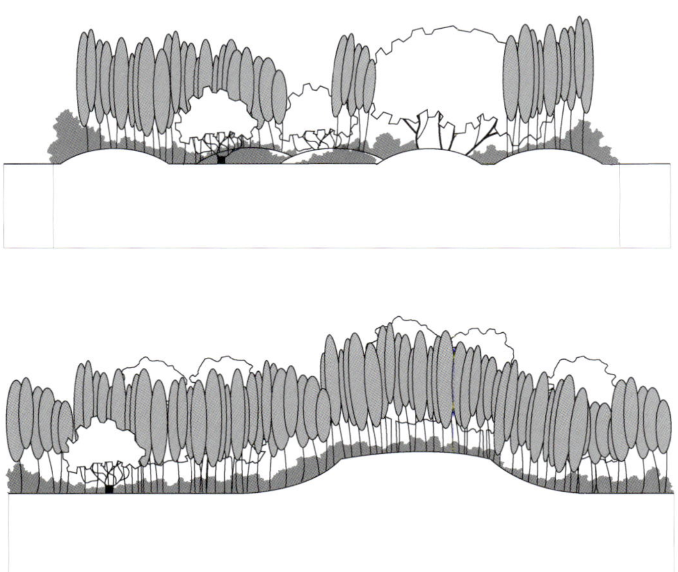

Clumps of Trees, Brushwood, Vegetation of Saplings, Shrubbery

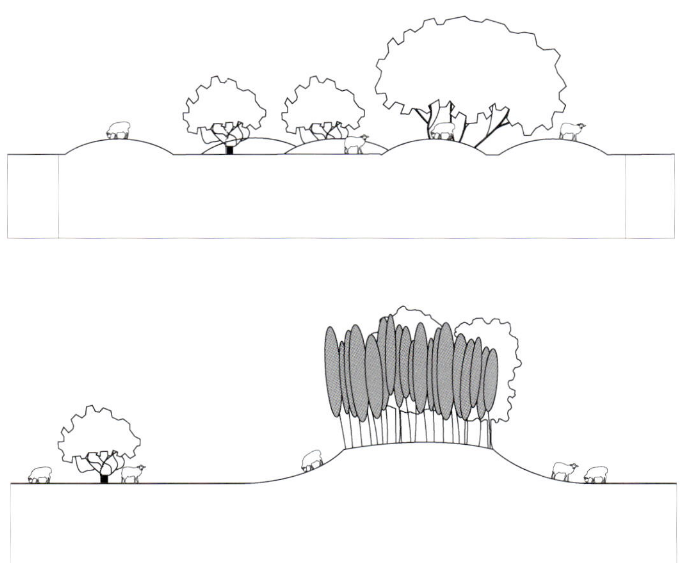

The uneven relief has been accentuated by specifically keeping more trees on the higher sections and less in the hollows

Top: Megalith grave

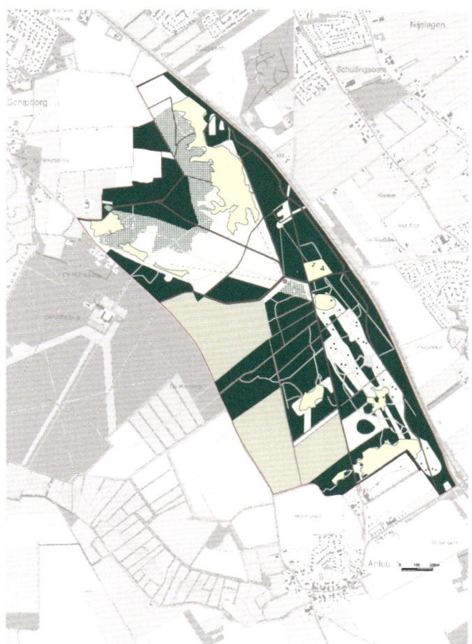

- Previous open places in the forest
- Future open places in the forest
- Future transparent forest
- Future forested areas
- Field/meadow

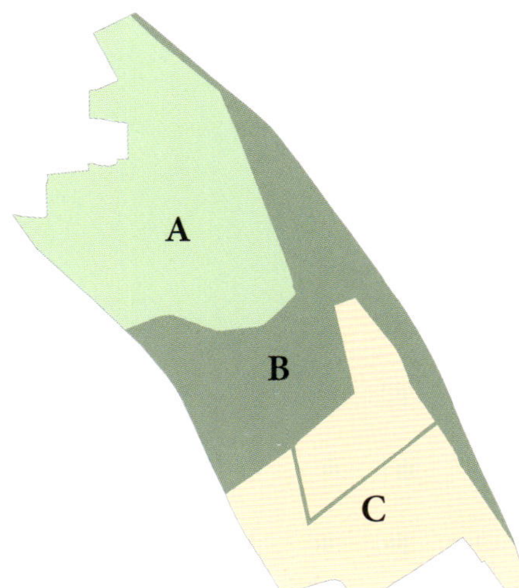

- **A** The Strubben area on the plateau of Schipborg
- **B** Reclaimed area (commercial forests and Kniphorstbosch)
- **C** Aeolian sands and heathland area with sandy depressions

Site Plan

1. Assault course
2. Shooting range
3. Bomb crater
4. Hollow driftway
5. Addersveentje (small lake)
6. Parabolic dune
7. Oak thickets
8. Strubbenweg (road)
9. Boekweitenveentje (small lake)
10. Bomb craters
11. Small lake (sacrificial place)
12. Hand grenade range with building/cellar
13. Trench
14. Galgenberg (hill)
15. Burial mound
16. Kniphorstbosch
17. Former site of the Villa Maria recognizable by the pond and the beech trees
18. De Berekuil depression
19. General's barrow
20. Bomb crater
21. Jerusalem depression
22. Bosweg (road)
23. Camping
24. Anloo church view
25. Depression at Anloo
26. Anloo despression view
27. Schipborgerweg (road)
28. Western Galgenbergweg (road)
29. Borgweg (road)
30. Northern Galgenbergweg (road)
31. Eastern Galgenbergweg (road)

Late neolothic burial mound, early and middle Bronze Age
Burial mound in late Bronze Age/early Iron Age
Tumulus in the late Iron Age
Middle neolithic megalith grave
Possible traces of Celtic field
Distinct cart tracks
Heathland
Ridge
Grassland with scarce heathland
Shifting sand area
Heathland with depression
Small pool/hollow
Field/meadow
Holt/wood
Old forest
Oak shrub vegetation
Forest with outdoor character
Seedbed forest
Production forest
Transparent production forest
Spontaneous forest
Avenue and wooded bank
Oaks placed out of line
Parking area
Visual relationship with environment
Former shooting range and assault course
(Bailey) bridge or underpass
Solitary tree

Top: Heath-land with grazing sheep, two months after execution of the design

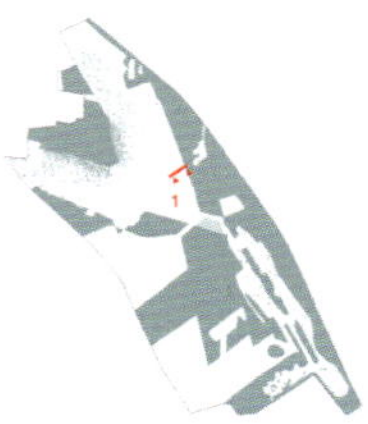

Present Situation

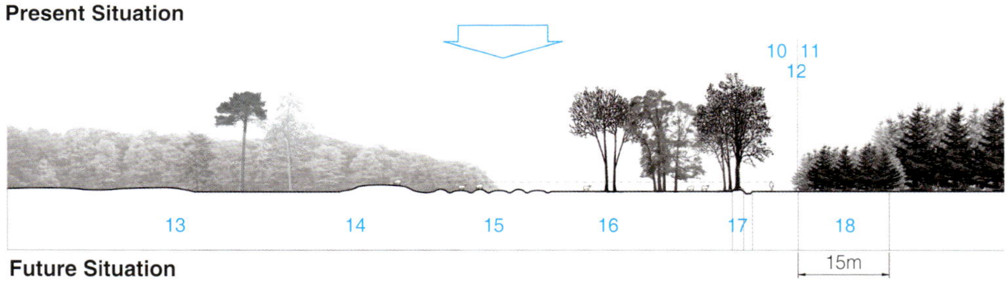

Future Situation

1. Conversion of spontaneous woodland to grazed open heath with a few solitary trees
2. Clearing of cart tracks=removal of deposits and undergrowth to make cart tracks visible
3. Thinning out of oaks along former marked boundary
4. Possible creation of a new tidy border of Norway spruce
5. Spontaneous wood with Scots pine, ordinary broad-leaf trees and undergrowth
6. Concealed cart tracks and sand ridges
7. Concealed cart tracks and sand ridges
8. Former marked boundary
9. Production wood with conifers
10. Inside
11. Outside
12. Grazing area
13. Open heath with a few solitary trees
14. Visible cart tracks and sand ridges
15. Visible cart tracks and sand ridges
16. Views toward strubben
17. Oaks
18. New tidy fringe visible from open heath

Artist's Impression: Transition from Production Wood to Shrub Heath

Top: Cleared oak shrubs after implementation of the design

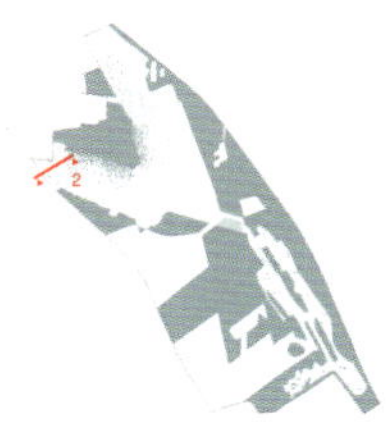

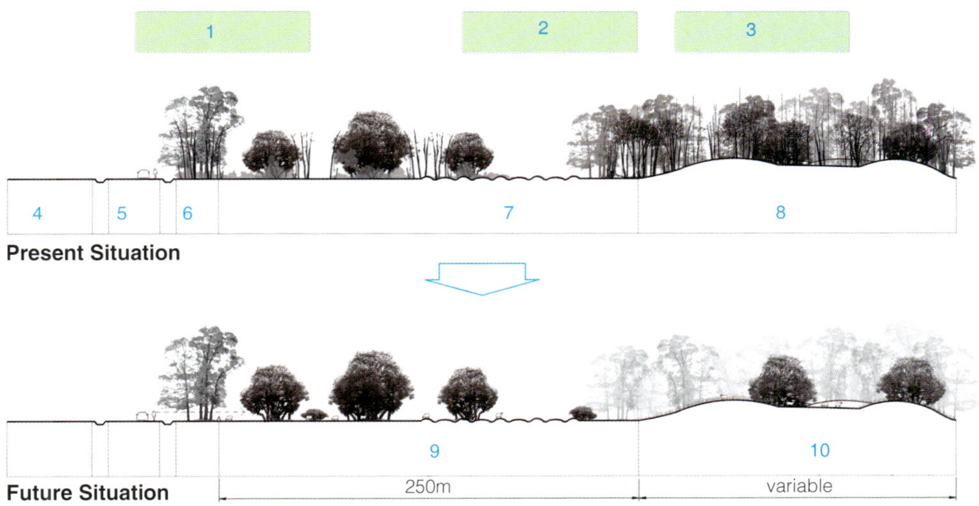

1. To thin-out fringe of oaks=removal of vegetation and undergrowth
2. Exempt oak shrubs=removal of undergrowth
3. Exempt Parabolic dune=leave only the oak shrubs and tree rings
4. Meadow
5. Schipborg-weg (road)
6. Oak fringe
7. Embraced by the Parabolic dune oak shrubs obstructed by competitors and cart tracks
8. Thick overgrown Parabolic dune
9. Embraced by the Parabolic dune: oak shrubs and tree rings coming out of new oak shrubs influenced by grazing and distinct cart tracks, and the coming about of a wealth of various grasslands through grazing/ mowing
10. Parabolic dune and the coming about of a wealth of various grasslands through grazing/ mowing

Artist's Impression: Hollow and Parabolic Dune with Thicket

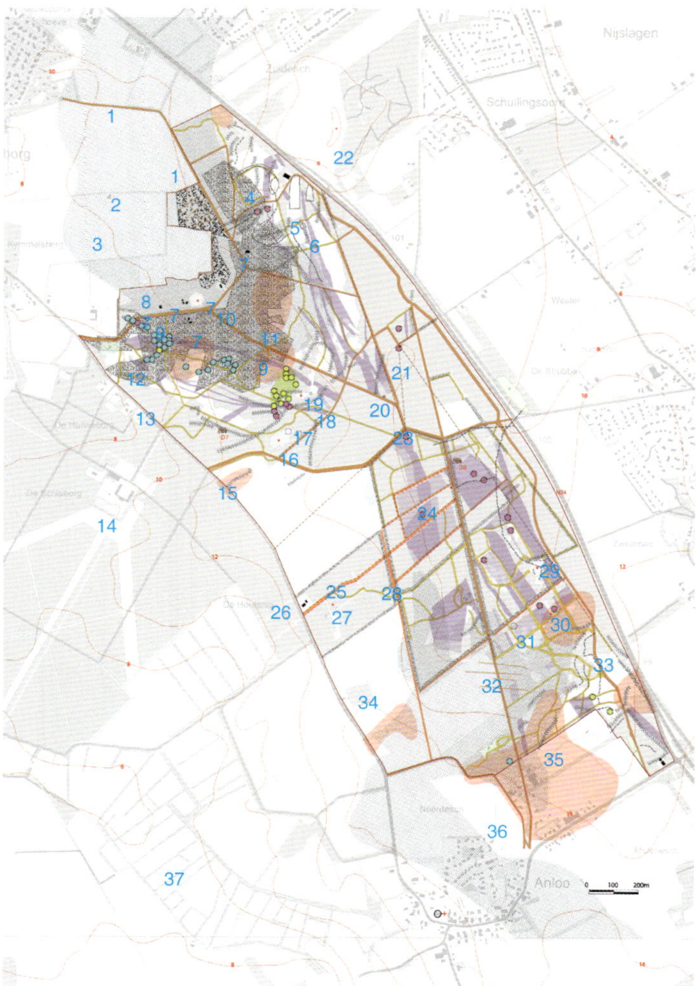

1. Hollow driftway
2. Esweg (road)
3. De Esch
4. Assault course
5. Shooting range
6. Bomb crater
7. Residence
8. De Koekoek
9. Strubbenweg (road)
10. Addersveentje (small lake)
11. Oak Thickets
12. Parabolic dune
13. Borgweg (road)
14. Kröller-Müller experimental farm
15. Schipborgerweg (road)
16. Boekweitenveentje (small lake)
17. Bomb craters
18. Small lake (sacrificial place)
19. Hand grenade range with building/cellar
20. Trench
21. Burial mound
22. Disappeared depression Borchermeer
23. Galgenberg (hill)
24. Game keeper's cottage which has disappeared, still recognisable by the beech trees and the cellar
25. Disappeared watch tower
26. Forest ranger's cottage from the 1920s
27. Former Villa Maria, recognisable by the pond and the beech trees
28. Kniphorstbosch
29. De Berekuil depression
30. General's barrow
31. Bomb crater
32. Bosweg (road)
33. Jerusalem depression
34. Old holding farm
35. Camping
36. Cemetery
37. Depression at Anloo

Axis hollow
Ridge
Peat depression (hollow with a surrounding bank)
Plateaus at Schipborg/Anloo
Urnfields/remaining urnfields
Settlement site
Late neolithic burial mound; early and middle Bronze Age
Burial mound in the late Bronze Age/early Iron Age
Tumulus in the late Iron Age
Middle neolithic megalith grave
Possible traces of celtic field
Holt/wood
Oakshrub vegetation
Parking area
Distinct cart tracks
Vague cart tracks

Above: Bomb crater after implementation of the design
Opposite top: The clearing of oak shrubs and the result after implementation of the design

Forest 1910 **Forest 1940** **Forest 1982** **Forest 2003** **Forest 2007** **Future Forest**

Mont Evrin Park

Location: Montévrain, France
Area: 20 hectares (49.42 acres)
Landscape Design: URBICUS Ltd/Jean-Marc Gaulier
Project Managers: Chrystelle Rouge, Bénédicte Morel, Clément Bollinger
Photography: Charles Delcourt and Michel Reuss
Clients: EPA Marne and City of Montévrain

This 20 hectares (49.42acres) park, developed on former farmland, is the backbone of the new Montévrain district in north-central France.

It is inspired by the rural landscape of the surrounding countryside, and features meadows, hedgerows, a small woodland area, and a vast wetland area to be used in the creation of a storm drain. Ultimately designed to be experienced as a natural space, the park remains flexible, evolving to the rhythm of differentiated management.

Mont Evrin Park is maintained by different management groups, and is part of a voluntary strategy to promote biodiversity and energy-saving. Only the verges by the paths are regularly mown, and the meadows are maintained in accordance with flowering times and visitor numbers. The ditches and hedgerows are designed as ecological corridors, planted with rustic and local species.

Set among housing, the Grand Verger (Great Orchard) offers the most garden-like environment in the park. Vast meadows, high and low, planted with flowering trees, form 'rooms' linked to inhabited islands. The central meadow ensures visual continuity across the orchard. Enclosed areas enable the cultivation of fruit trees, currant bushes, and hazelnut trees, where walkers can pick fruit and nuts.

Continuing on from the Grand Verger, the small wood and hedged farmland create a rural environment in the park. Meadows planted with standard fruit trees follow on from a moorland area covered with broom, then give way to a young forest. To save resources and promote natural competition between plants, enclosures of forest plants form the basis of the little wood-to-be.

The furniture, which is custom-designed, is part of a simple and rustic range that is durable and low-maintenance. Dotted throughout the park and in keeping with the ground materials, it is accompanied by lecterns and signs telling walkers about the various environments and management of the park.

To enable the town council departments and residents to understand the environments of the park and take ownership, a voluntary communication and education strategy has been implemented, explaining the park's management and philosophy. Graphic documents tailored to different audiences (e.g. signs, lecterns, leaflets, explanation notices) have been made by the project management team with the assistance of an illustrator, author, and graphic designers.

Top: The atmospheres are fed of the rural landscapes of the surrounding countryside
Bottom: Access to a mineral small place
Opposite top: The park remains flexible, evolving at the rate of the differentiated management

The Montévrain District

Top: The orchard is open to park visitors
Bottom: In summer, people occupy the lawns
Opposite top: A seating area in a meadow setting

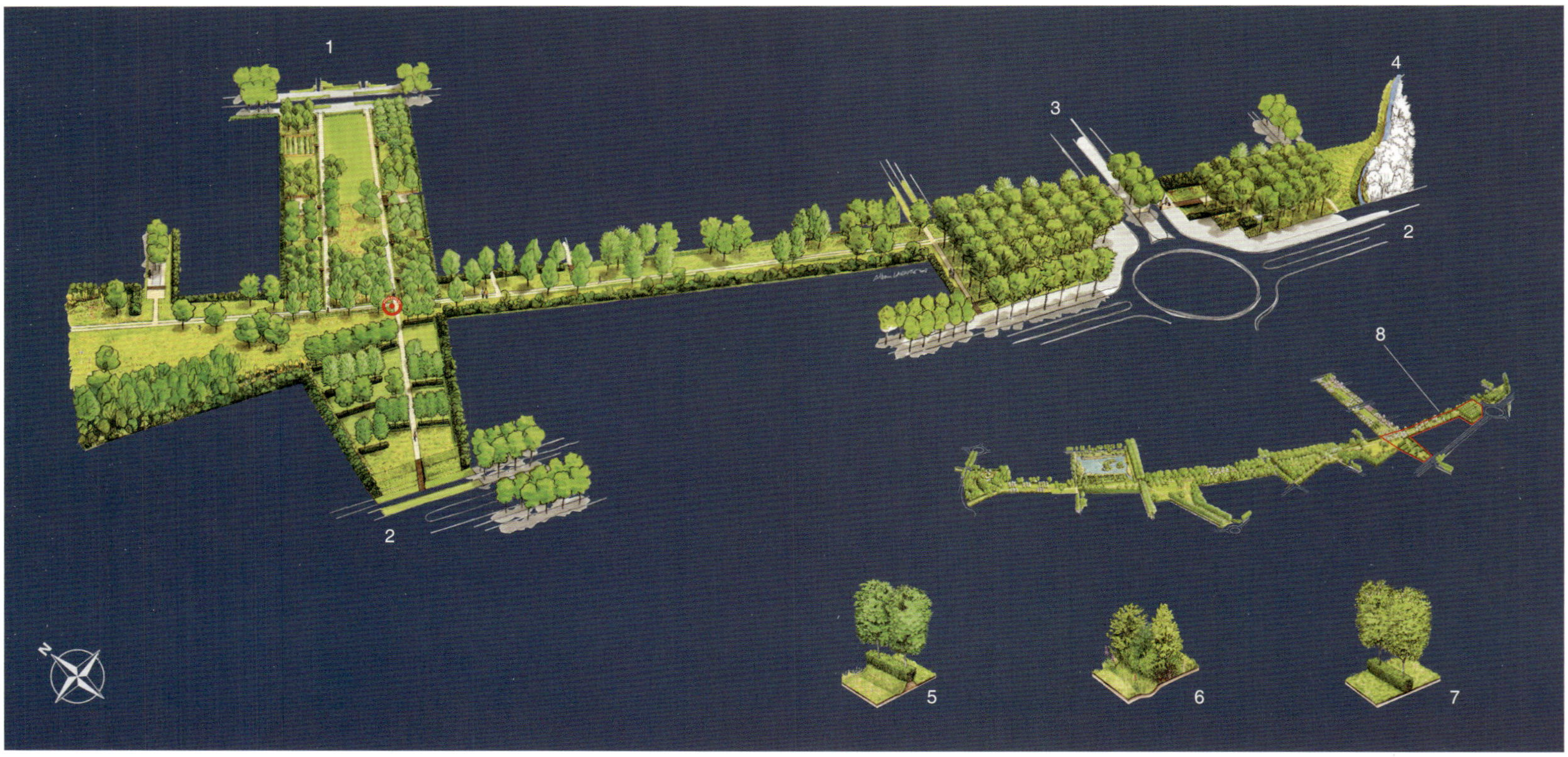

1. Avenue of the League of Nations
2. RD 231
3. Avenue of Europe
4. Gasset Street
5. Hedges on a slope
6. Small forest area
7. Trimmed hedges
8. Tourism activities

Top left: Access to the park
Top righ: Flowery meadow in spring
Opposite top: A bench near the orchard
Opposite middle and bottom: The park is enjoyed year-round by local residents

Norges River

Location: Norges-la-Ville, France
Area: 1254 square meters (13498 square feet)
Landscape Design: TERRITOIRES Landscape Architects
Photography: Nicolas Waltefaugle © NWPHOTO.fr
Client: City of Norges-la-Ville

The richness and depth of Norges-la-Ville, a french village near Dijon, France, is bonded to the natural source of the Norges River. Depending on the season, the zone around the river was often inaccessible, depriving locals of the stunning beauty of this landscape. The purpose of this project was to rehabilitate the wet meadows nearby and enlarge the space around the river.

A large wooden deck—a terrace over the river itself—is the starting point for the newly-developed river walkway.

A pedestrian boardwalk, designed like a wharf on wooden stilts (made from oak), leaves the domesticated space and crosses a symbolic border.

The meadow zone is extremely wet, and when the river overflows its banks transform the area into temporary swamps. The transition between these two areas, from domesticated to wild and unpredictable, is where the magic truly happens.

An elevated access was necessary. The boardwalk carries visitors into this fantasy land without ever touching the ground, creating this levitation feeling. This choice is respectful to the ecosystem, encourages wildlife, and also offers a technical answer to keeping the pathway accessible when the river overflows.

The wharf is crossed by some branching accessways, bringing new perspectives into this poetic journey, while a wooden bridge over the river invites contemplation.

The geometric contrast plays an important part as well, mirroring the river's natural sinuous curves with the boardwalk's radical lines.

With minimal man-made intrusion, this landscape is finally re-discovered, and served with an out-of-reality, undisturbed aesthetic.

Top and bottom: Wooden path along the Norges River
Opposite top: The Norges River

Top: The wooden path set alongside the river
Bottom: The river setting invites exploration via an intimate path
Opposite: Footbridge crossing the River Norges

Top, bottom and opposite: Wooden path and grassland

The Meadow Park

Location: Giessen, Germany
Area: 42 hectares (103.78 acres)
Landscape Design: A24 Landschaft Landschaftsarchitektur GmbH
Photography: Hanns Joosten
Client: City of Giessen

The university town of Giessen has rediscovered the banks of the Lahn River, exposing the urban development potential it had long neglected, with its the central river banks, meadows, and adjacent urban quarters. The framework plan by A24 Landschaft, adopted in 2011, developed the shores of the Lahn into a completely new and multifaceted inner-city recreational area. Implementation was carried out in phases, as the various spaces become available.

The river has long been thought of as purely functional, and wasused accordingly. The 1849 construction of the railroad—with its high embankment alongside the river—effectively severed any inner-city access to the river landscape. As a result, the river meadows formed an inner-city periphery comprising of many inaccessible areas, some of which are used extensively, while others are used less frequently or as vast parking areas. Only with the Eparadigm of uniting cities with their rivers did Giessen's potential become fully recognized.

The long-term Lahnaue Framework Plan encompasses the entire inner-city river basin, while it is dictated by the overall concept of connecting the Lahn to the city. The plan envisions six segments: from the open and extensive grassland park in the north, through the more densely urbanized areas in and around the inner city, and stretching to the natural ensemble of existing river meadows in the

Lahnäue Framework Plan

south. The segments are connected by a new, continuous path running along both banks of the Lahn.

The plan also entails the removal of parking along the riverside, unsealing the areas, as well as renewing and expanding the existing parks. The idea is to develop connections between the segments, establish public squares, and extend cross-regional bicycle paths to reach the Lahn. Not least, the concept reclaims private property along the river for public use, while initiating revegetation processes and measures for long-term preservation of the riverscape.

The city of Giessen used the 2014 State Garden Show and the public interest it aroused to implement the first two measures of the framework plan.

The first project is a new entrance to the city in the central urban area of the framework plan. The entrance—'By the Mills'—includes a representative square, a new boulevard, an elaborate mill garden, and varyingly designed approaches to the water. Across from the square lies the large meadow playground, which occupies the site of a former parking lot. The playground invites children of all ages to play on four differentiated play terraces. These also reference the river theme, emulating typical elements of a meadow landscape.

The second project is a new pedestrian and bicycle bridge at the northern part of the city. It now constitutes one of three bridges in Giessen that cross the river, and has greatly improved the city's infrastructure. The new bridge has also allowed for the implementation of the first part of the extensive meadow park envisioned in the framework plan.

Particular emphasis was placed on planting extensive vegetation that would require minimal maintenance. A decision was made to cultivate native wetlands that required mowing only twice each year,

Top and opposite top: Pedestrian and bicycle bridge in the northern part of the city

and that provide a rich habitat for animals. The area along the water was revitalized with the planting of indigenous trees and aquatic vegetation that require no specific maintenance.

For purposes of stormwater management and flood control, the shore embankments were removed, the sealed areas loosened, and the entire banks lowered, allowing the wetlands to serve as a retention zone during peak flooding. Only the entrance squares connecting the park with the urban realm are raised and remain dry during flooding. All rainwater in the project zone is seeped locally to avoid overburdening the water network.

With the gradual implementation of additional goals from the framework plan, the city of Giessen, which had literally turned its back on its river, gained a new urban spatial orientation, and a new inner-city recreational area.

Section Meadow Playground

Top: Meadow park
Bottom: City entrance 'By the Mills'
Opposite top: Wooden deck in the mill garden
Opposite bottom: Seating by the river

Top: Meadow playground with installations for children
Bottom left and right: Small basin and children's entertainment facilities in the playground
Opposite top: Mill Garden surrounded by several buildings with some small trees
Opposite bottom: The lawn and long benches in the Mill Garden

Punggol Promenade

Location: Singapore
Area: 8.23 hectares (20.34 acres)
Landscape Design: LOOK Architects Pte Ltd
Photography: LOOK Architects Pte Ltd
Client: Urban Redevelopment Authority

Punggol Promenade is a waterfront landscape set within the surrounding urban setting, allowing visitors to revel in a poetic interlude of intertwining shifting planes of time and space. Memories of a bygone era are evoked through the embodiment of signifiers, and reality melds with processes of familiarization to yield new layers of meaning. The experience becomes so immersive and personal that a comforting sense of reconciliation with nature is inspired.

The expansiveness of water and sky seen from Punggol Point beach seems to stretch infinitely, obliterating the nearby towering neighborhood of public housing, as the linearity of the safety railing sitting on black pigmented concrete plinths coaxes the eyes to be led toward the horizon. The severity of this bold color treatment carries undertones of sobriety in tribute to Punggol Point beach as a World War II memorial site, a sliver of history that is otherwise little known. One may see the viewing deck overlooking Punggol Point beach as bearing resemblance to the hull of oil tankers dotting the surrounding waters, but its piercingly sharp silhouette may echo the scathing wounds of war for another.

Composition of materials applied throughout the 4.9km (3 mile) long promenade make up a rich palette, recalling the rustic character of old Punggol, a district which used to be populated with rural 'kampong' communities keeping farms and plantations. Richly

saturated hues of porous pebble, oxidized steel, and laterite speak of a genuine, down-to-earth honesty that endears to the uprooted instability of urbanized society, while the weathered texture of simulated GRC (glass fiber reinforced concrete) timber planks instills a continual tactility along the meandering pedestrian path.

Interspersed along the promenade are sculpturally-shaped rest shelters offering much-welcomed respite from the tropical heat. A steel structure in aluminum cladding, the rest shelter is shaped as a dynamic swirling form that draws inspiration from elements of the coastal context, emulating the rolling sea waves and the corkscrew shell. The external cladding is configured out of a single triangulated module, which through calculated permutation adopts the distinctive geometry. Versatility of this configuration has been demonstrated in the semi-enclosed envelop of the rest shelter, a design consideration safeguarding against anti-social behavior. The armor-like envelope will develop a weathered patina over time, the character of which will meld with the down-to-earth charm of the promenade. Inner faces of the shelter—interlocking trapezoidal aluminum panels strengthening the envelop—have a soft sheen which captures the ambient mood of surroundings by reflecting the changing hues of light throughout the day.

Poetic speculation on man-made artifice and nature is inspired by calculated framing—whether glancing upon a lily pond by the seaside, or hovering close to the water's edge on a cantilevered look-out platform—to rouse an invigorated connection to landscape and nature.

Top: Rest area along the sea
Opposite top: The beach at sunset

1. Johor Strait
2. Dam
3. Future housing deveopment
4. Coney Island
5. Punggol waterway development
6. Serangoon Reservoir
7. Lorong Halus Wetland
8. Pulau Ubin
9. Punggol walk
10. Nature walk
11. Riverside walk

Top: Bench with arched awnings
Opposite: Wooden deck along the water

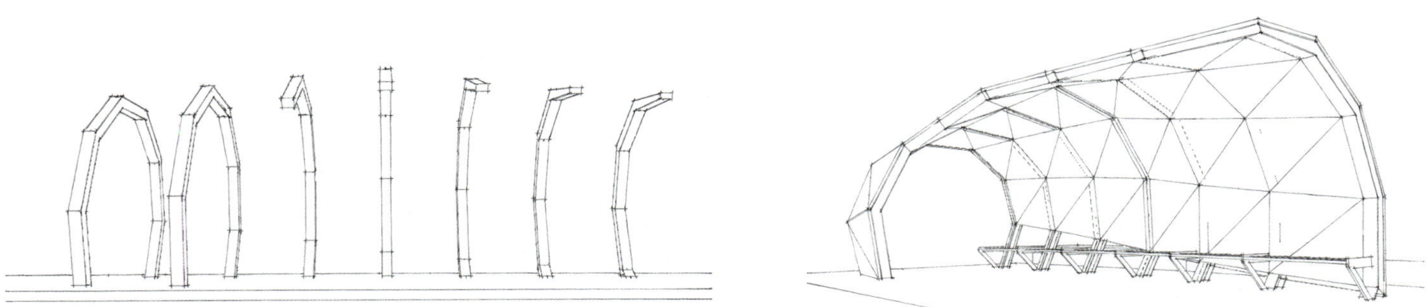

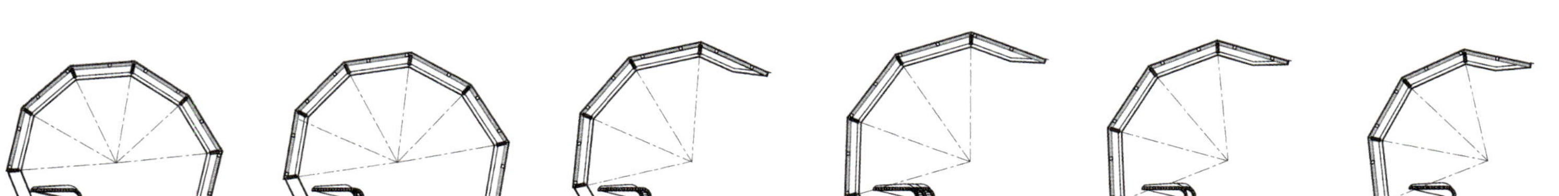

Elevation Plan

Top: Huge pool
Middle right: Mottled metal wall
Bottom right: A bridge across the water

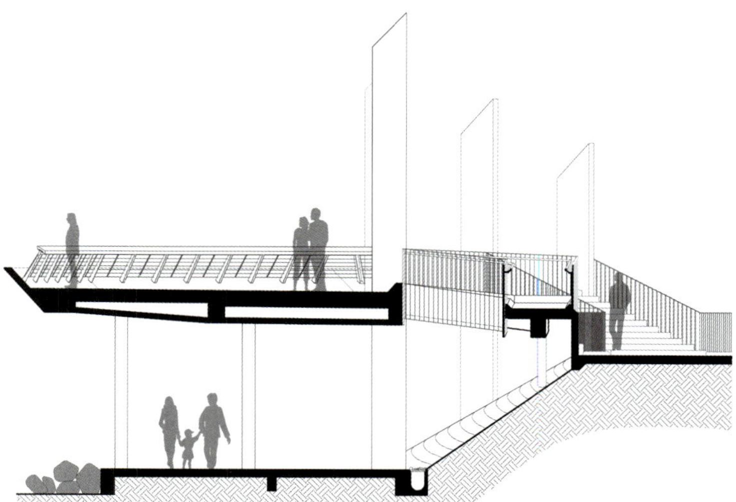

Elevation Plan

Top: Rest place with chairs, which are surrounded by lush vegetation

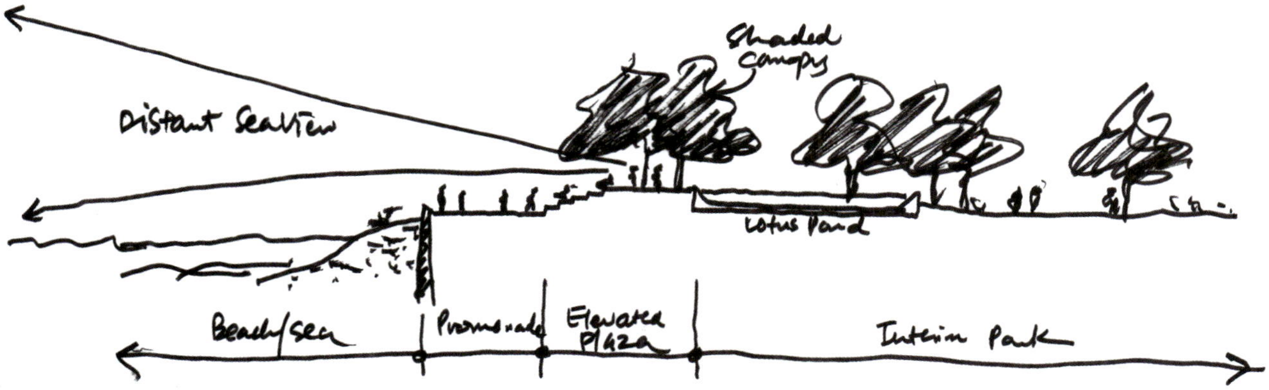

Sketch

Ballooërveld

Location: Drentsche Aa area, Netherlands
Area: 800 hectares (1976.84 acres)
Landscape Design: Strootman Landschapsarchitecten
Photography: Harry Cock
Client: North Netherlands Forestry Commission
Partners: University of Groningen (Theo Spek and Jeroen Zomer) and Hans Elerie

Ballooërveld is the largest remaining heath in the Drentsche Aa area near Groningen in the Netherlands.

The gradient from the heath to the low-lying ground through which the brooks wind, along with the accumulation of archaeological, historico-geographical, historico-ecological, and geological values, make the Ballooërveld an area of exceptional natural beauty.

The land had been the property of the Forestry Commission for some time; the field itself was used as a terrain for military exercises before it was transferred to the Forestry Commission by the Ministry of Defence.

All interested parties and experts collaboratively drew up a redesign and management plan for the Ballooërveld, with an emphasis on optimal enjoyment of the historical and ecological qualities and the large open space.

The Ballooërveld is like an old skin full of scars in the form of wagon tracks, Celtic fields, barrow mounds, an anti-tank ditch, a trench, windbreaks, wooded banks, water discharges, and reclamations. The removal of vertical vegetation made it easier to see the spatial coherence between these elements.

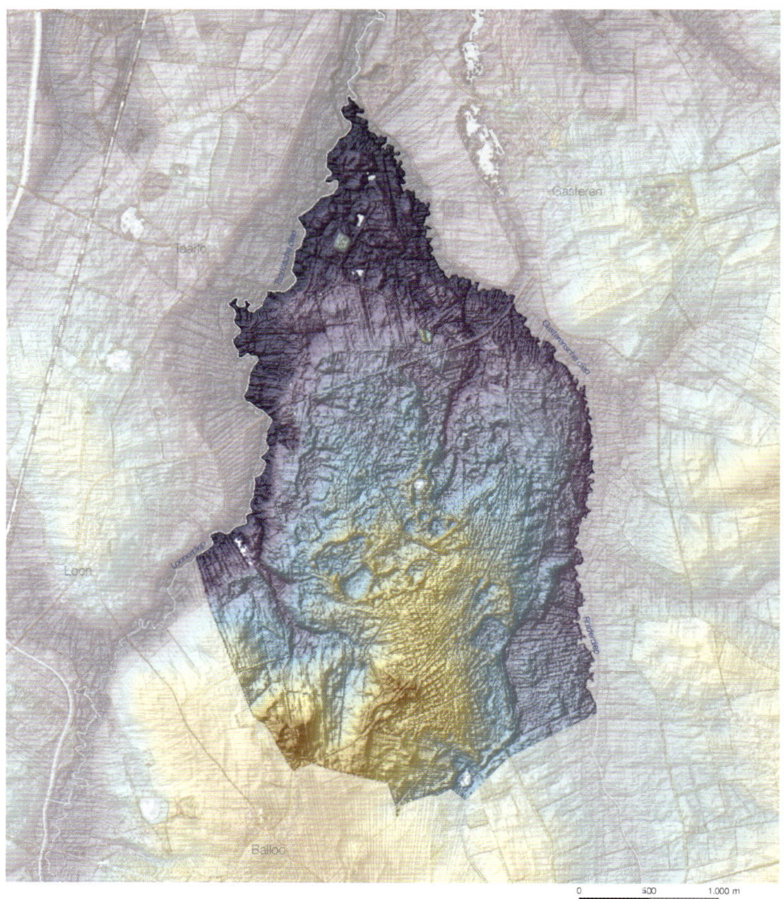

Elevation Map of the Ballooërveld

Top: The vast wilderness vegetation
Bottom: Yellow land and red vegetation coexistence in harmony

At some points there are small reclamations on the large, peaceful heath that are bordered by a wooded bank and have thus come to lie on the open heath like striking islands. Solitary trees and small clusters of trees remain. Thanks to the large degree of variation in the landscape, the perspective for visitors changes at every turn.

Design Concept at Different Angles

Top: Long and narrow road for cycling
Middle and bottom: Desert landscape before the reconstruction
Opposite top: Burial mound after execution of the design

1

2

3

4

5

6

The Habitats of Red-Listed Species be Improved

1. Gentiana pneumonanthe
2. Phengaris alcon
3. Plebejus argus
4. Saxicola rubicola
5. Rana arvalis
6. Vipera berus

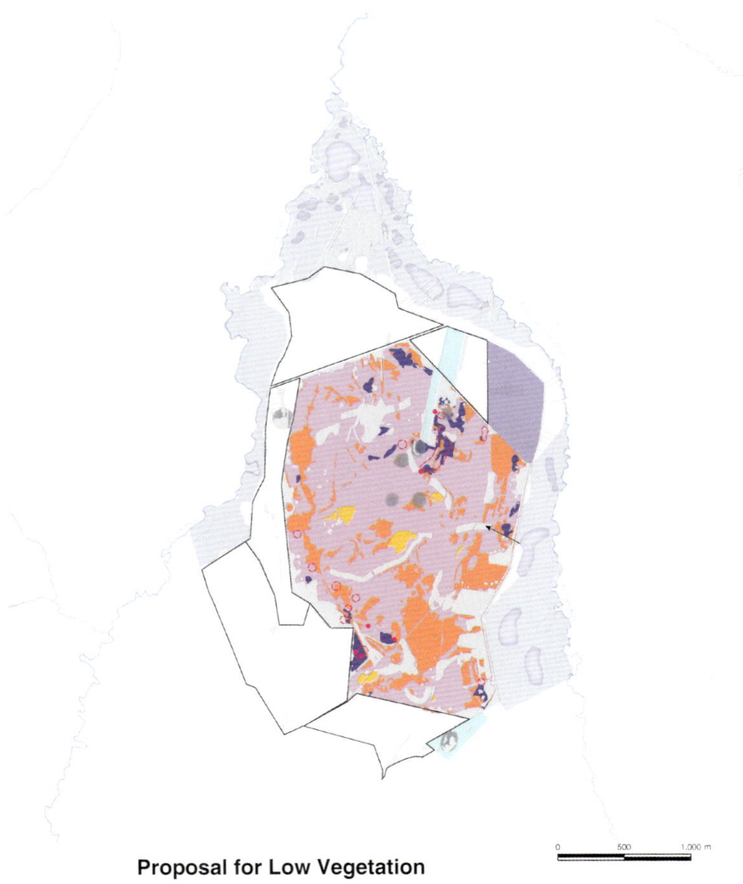

Proposal for Low Vegetation

Maintain, Add and Remove Vegetation

Top: Blooming lavender
Bottom left: Lush vegetation
Bottom right: 'Heerenweg' (path) through the heath and burial mounds after execution of the design
Opposite top: Cart tracks through the heath and view of a church in Rolde

Top and opposite top: Desert landscape set off under the setting sun, allowing visitors to experience the endless charm of nature

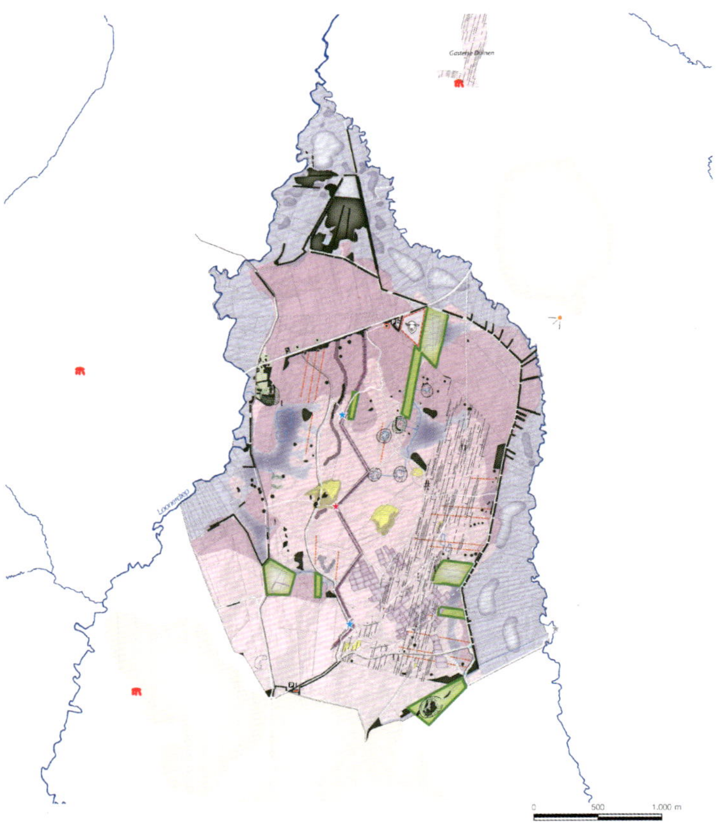

Site Plan

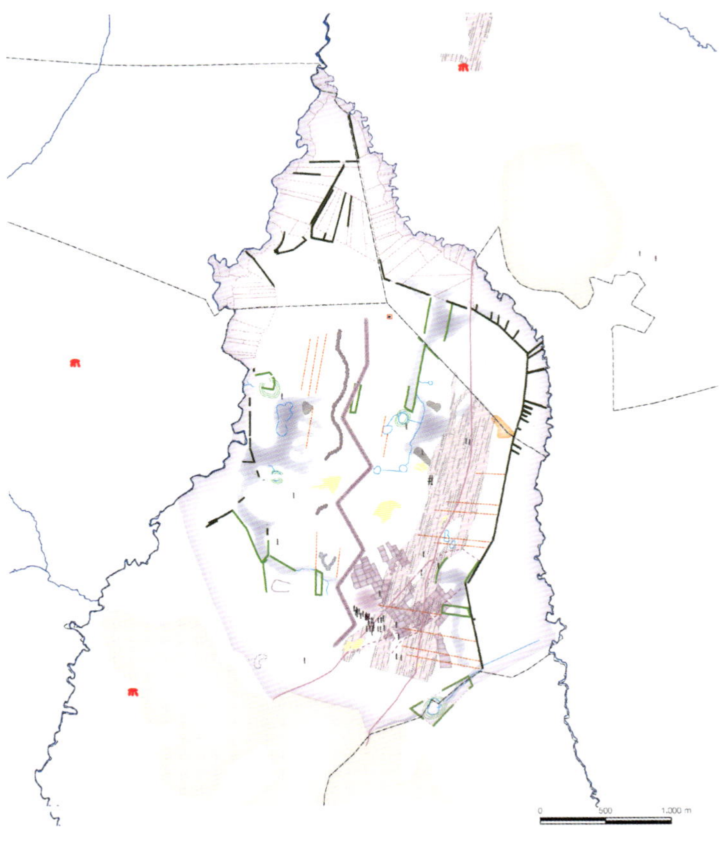

Map With Relics from Different Periods

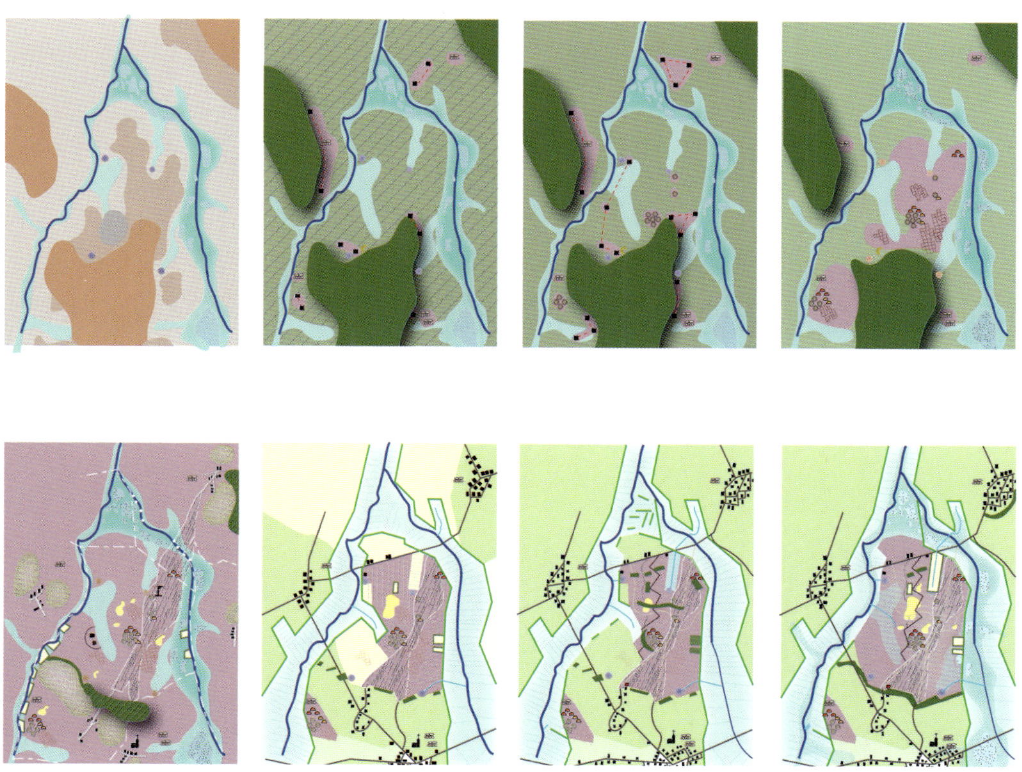

The Development of the Ballooërveld Since Approximately 8000 BC Until Now

North Diaoyutai Development

Location: Beijing, China
Area: 4000 square meters (43055 square feet)
Landscape Design: Martha Schwartz Partners
Photography: Fei Qi
Client: Beijing Changshi Oriental Land

Martha Schwartz Partners (MSP) were commissioned by Beijing Changshi Oriental Land to produce a landscape vision for the North Diaoyutai Development at Yanqi (Swan) Lake, 50-kilometer (31 miles) north of Beijing, China.

The vision was for an immersive landscape framework, one that wraps the built components of the project within a unifying environment, tying together varied architectural styles into one coherent whole. In addition to the overall landscape vision, MSP is responsible for the detailed design of a number of areas within the project, including Fanqi Road (the street address of the project), the Southern and Northern Residential entries, and the Shore Garden.

Fanqi Road is a 340-meter (1115-foot) long diorama—a contemporary interpretation of a Chinese landscape painting. The landscape rises away from the road in a series of extruded stone boxes; a 'mountain' stepping up and protecting the North Diaoyutai project.

These boxes form planters for native trees, shrubs, and bamboo plants. The boxes also form 'plinths' for the exhibition of Chinese geology in the form of massive rocks. Water runs from the central hotel entrance downhill to the south and north, cascading down the stone plinths and running into the development as a symbol of vitality and wealth.

The Renders from Different Angles

The Shore Garden is a place of peace and Zen. Nestled at the foot of the Tadao Ando Hotel, the shore garden is home to five amazing spa spaces—each a pavilion secluded in woodland. The woodland frames the main axis of the spa garden, which is dominated by a series of water mirrors. These mirrors are 'floating' steel sheets over which water flows. The arrangement of these mirrors is a calculated optical illusion—the plan arrangement of these objects causes false perspective; when viewed from the hotel the effect is of a continuous sheet of water. For the select few who can inhabit the shore garden, it is possible to move between the water mirrors and experience them 'up close'. When the mist rolls in from Fanqi Lake, the landscape surface below the water mirrors will be shrouded—only the 'impossibly' thin water mirrors are seen, effortlessly floating above the morning mist.

Top: The panorama of North Diaoyutai Development from the road
Opposite top: Small bamboo trees standing on the side of the road

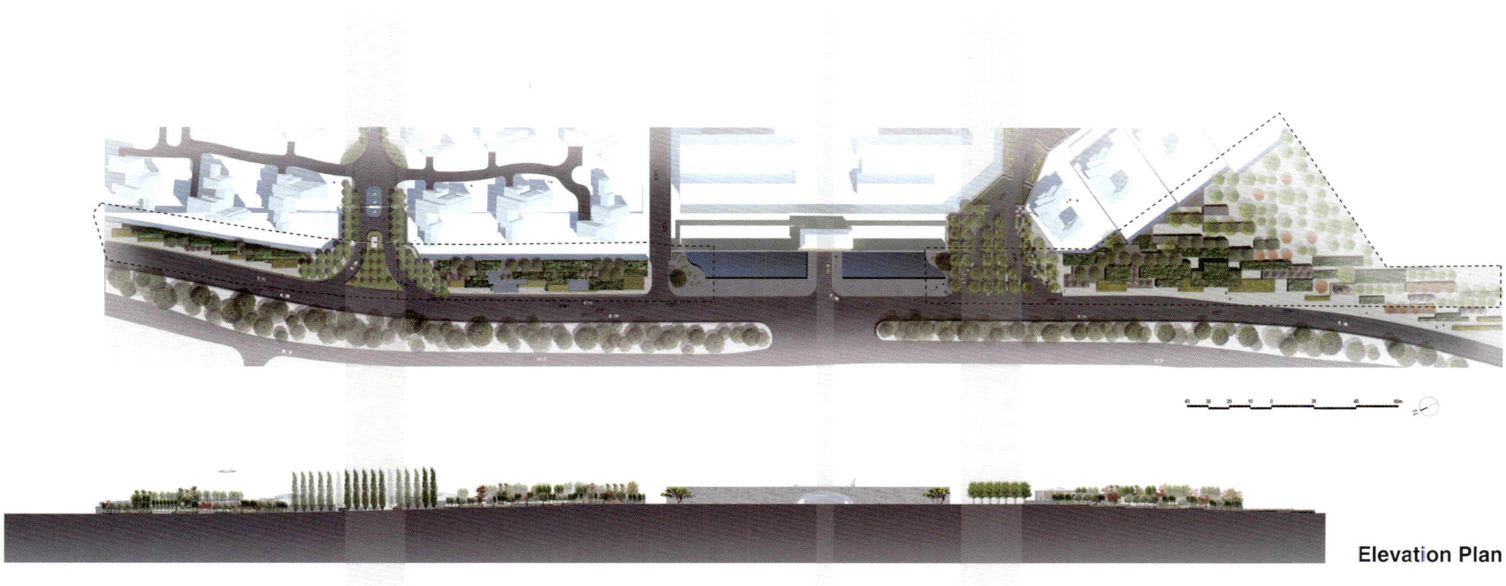

Elevation Plan

Top: The flower beds made from grey stones
Opposite top: A long and narrow water feature

Renders of the Landscape Along the Road

Stereoscopic Landscape Renders

Leisure Centre of Madine's Lake

Location: Lorraine, France
Area: 30 hectares (74.13 acres)
Landscape Design: URBICUS Ltd/Jean-Marc Gaulier
Architecture Design: 2AD Ltd/Lucie Rivault
Project Managers: Thomas Boisdet & Claire Bellet
Photography: URBICUS Ltd/Demathieu & Bard
Client: Région Lorraine/Union of Madine Lake

Madine Lake is one of the largest lakes in France, with expansive forests spread along its banks and shores. A leisure and tourism center sat at the heart of the lake in Madine, but over time had fallen into disuse.

The aim of this redevelopment project was to therefore create a new facility on the site with a distinctive identity and sense of structure.

The original layout consisted of a road set back from the shore, which was used by both pedestrians and service vehicles. This organization created discontinuity in the route and fragmentation of the space, particularly access to meadows by the lakeshore.

Going against this original layout, the idea behind the redevelopment was to create one single facility, unitary and homogeneous, with elements of the scheme incorporated into a public nature park accessible to all.

The new facility incorporates a broad range of amenities, including those for leisure activities (playgrounds, beach, reception building) and water sports (harbor master's office, dry dock, pier for pleasure boats), and also diversifies the commercial offering, with a restaurant, bar, and kiosks.

Top: Aerial view of the leisure center and harbor

The leisure center was designed around a new boardwalk design. At once a building, square, and promenade, it has become the symbol of the area's regeneration. The surrounding landscape, made up of woodlands, wetlands, and vast meadows, is an exceptional and very well preserved natural heritage site.

One of the main ideas of the project was to create a walkway that enters into a dialogue with the lake, offers a variety of viewpoints, and constitutes a new way of understanding the landscape of the lake.

A monumental wooden sculpture, the grand deck is a dash of modernity. Its relief highlights the topography of the site; its undulations shelter the buildings, and its recesses offer space for water activities. A public space that structures the site, as a town square or large mall would in a city, the leisure center is a place for walking and meeting.

The boardwalk is for leisure and activity, and encompasses the entire length and breadth of the site. Walking paths stretch from the countryside all the way into the water via landing stages that dot the lakeside, thus creating links between the village and the lake.

Top: The boardwalk
Middle: The great meadow, terraced by two Corten lines
Bottom: Tables and barbecues designed by Vincent Dupont-Rougier
Opposite top: Harbor square; in the background, the harbor master's office
Opposite bottom left: The reception building—a bridge offers a panoramic view over the lake
Opposite bottom right: Oak wood deck climbs over the roof of the building

Top: Pier for public pleasure boats
Bottom left: The boardwalk
Bottom right: Picnic area
Opposite top: The beach and its aid station
Opposite bottom: Beach, jetty, and pontoons for swimmers

POSTE DE SECOURS

Index

A24 Landschaft Landschaftsarchitektur GmbH | 60, 134, 196

Web: www.a24-landschaft.com
Tel: 030 311 69 64 0
Fax: 030 311 69 64 99

The projects of A24 Landschaft Landschaftsarchitektur GmbH are predominantly found in the urban realm, at the interface between landscape and the built city. The objective, spanning urban development and individual properties, is the rich harmonization of buildings with exterior structures. The design of urban squares, promenades, and pedestrian zones is the focus of the practice.

The point of departure for the work at A24 Landschaft is always the location, with its unique qualities that are singled out and developed. This conceptual intervention clarifies, intensifies, and strengthens the location.

The team comprises 20 architects and landscape architects working on several public projects and competitions in the fields of landscape architecture and urban development on a variety of different of scales.

Archiplanstudio | 20, 142

Web: www.archiplanstudio.com
Tel: (+39) 0376 324525
Fax: (+39) 0376 324525

Since its development in 1997, Archiplanstudio has designed public buildings; private, residential, and commercial dealings; and local projects that enhance the landscape. It is active in the field of interior design and fittings. Each project represents an opportunity for Archiplanstudio. The research focuses on the ability that has the architecture to translate and express themes and relationships. The study is not concerned with the question of style as a system of recognizability of the author, but the studio is interested in the potentiality that owns the project, intended as a process, and the final summary that reveals figures, forms, and spaces.

Diego Cisi graduated in Venice in architectural design with highest honors. Since 1999 he has been teaching at universities. He is teacher at the Politecnico di Milano, and is consultant for areas subject to landscape for several municipalities of the province of Mantua.

Stefano Gorni Silvestrini graduated in Venice in architectural design with highest honors. Since 2000 he has been teaching at the Politecnico di Milano. He is a consultant for areas subject to landscape for several municipalities of the province of Mantua.

Blackwell & Associates | 120

Web: www.blackwell.com.au
Add: 550 Stirling Hwy, Peppermint Grove, Western Australia, Australia, 6011
Tel: (08) 9383 0888

Blackwell & Associates was established in 1987. They are a specialized design practice focusing on sustainable landscape architecture and urban design solutions. Much of their focus since the practice was first established has been on the urban environment and on how they can enhance the experience when people trade their 'traditional' suburban existence for a higher density urban lifestyle.

A strong focus of their practice is in creating environments with a high level of pedestrian amenity, with a strong focus on streetscapes and on public open spaces offering high levels of aesthetic and physical appeal. They believe that their streetscapes should be conceived and developed as a natural extension of the Public Open Space network. It is their intent to improve their 'walkability', with an aim of encouraging more people to walk and ride and thereby deal with a number of current pressing health and environmental issues, as well as encouraging greater social interaction.

Bureau B+B | 114

Web: www.bplusb.nl
Add: Gedempt Hamerkanaal 96, 1021 KR Amsterdam, The Netherlands
E-mail: bureau@bplusb.nl

Bureau B+B is an urban and landscape architecture practice founded in 1977, with both national and international clients. They believe in collective talent, and in the shared intelligence of all bureau members. They start the design process by determining what makes the task unique and by identifying the elements the site offers. They then create a functional design that always includes an idea or an unsettling intervention that raises the spatial experience far beyond the simply functional.

In Bureau B+B's approach, perfection in craft and technique is guaranteed from the very first brainstorming session. Collaboration with clients is based on trust and communality. This offers room for flexible input in terms of scenarios, intermediate stages, and final images. Sustainability is their fifth core value, which summarizes their philosophy at the same time. The concept of ecological sustainability can be also applied to the built environment. In an urban context, sustainability means creating and maintaining a robust system of public spaces that are recognizable and fit the character of the city. Social sustainability is concerned with the quality of life and the social quality of a site—urban spaces change, but the challenge is for them to remain recognizable and familiar to their inhabitants.

GHD | 162

Web: www.ghd.com
Add: 16 Marcus Clarke Street, Canberra, ACT2601, Australia
Tel: +61 2 6113 3200

GHD is one of the world's leading professional services companies operating in the global markets of water, energy and resources, environment, property and buildings, and transportation. They provide engineering, architecture, environmental, and construction services to private and public sector clients.

Established in 1928 and privately owned, GHD operates across five continents—Asia, Australia, Europe, and North and South America—and the Pacific region. They employ more than 8500 people in 200+ offices to deliver projects with high standards of safety, quality, and ethics across the entire asset value chain. Driven by a client-service led culture, they connect the knowledge, skill, and experience of their employees with innovative practices, technical capabilities, and robust systems to create lasting community benefits.

Committed to sustainable development, GHD improves the physical, natural, and social environments of the many communities in which they operate.

Jeavons Landscape Architects | 154

Web: www.jeavons.net.au
Add: 1st Floor, 717 Nicholson Street, Carlton North, VIC 3054, Australia
Tel: +61 03 9387 7337

Jeavons Landscape Architects is a professional landscape architectural practice with extensive experience in the planning, design, and construction management of playspaces and landscapes for early learning centers, primary schools, secondary schools, special schools, aged-care facilities, community projects, residential developments, public parks, public spaces, and revegetation projects.

They work with a broad range of clients including local government; early childhood centers from both the public and private sectors; public and independent schools; architects on a variety of projects; and specialist clients including zoos and botanical gardens.

Les Jardiniers Nomades | 106

Web: www.lesjardiniersnomades.com
E-mail: lesjardiniersnomades@gmail.com

Les Jardiniers Nomades is a professional architecture and landscape design company. Four passionate young architects make up the company, including Michael de Tourdonnet, Arnaud Mermet Gerlat, Florian Michel, and Stanislas Bah Chuzeville. All come from rural backgrounds, so their projects are full of rustic sensibilities.

LOOK Architects Pte Ltd. | 204

Web: www.lookarchitects.com
Add: 18 Boon Lay Way, Singapore 609966
Tel: +65 6316 8676

LOOK Architects is a multi-award winning practice committed to rigorous analysis and research to produce innovative, iconic buildings and urban design. Embracing local sensibilities with a global outlook, LOOK Architects has garnered international acclaim for consistent achievements in design excellence—principal architect Look Boon Gee is the recipient of the prestigious President's Design Award Singapore 2009—Design of the Year, while the firm has received recognition from The Chicago Athenaeum for its efforts in both civic building and urban landscape design. Establishing a prolific and wide-ranging portfolio including high-rise condominium, mixed-use developments, varsity institutions, waterfront promenades, bridges and a public library, LOOK Architects strives to bring about innovation on projects of various scales and programmatic demands.

Martha Schwartz Partners | 222

Web: www.marthaschwartz.com
Add: 65-69 East Road, London N1 6AH, United Kingdom
Tel: 44 (0)20 7549 7497

Martha Schwartz Partners (MSP) is a leading international design practice whose work focuses on activating and regenerating urban sites and city centers. Situated at the intersection of landscape, art, and urbanism, MSP has over 30 years of experience designing and implementing installations, gardens, civic plazas, parks, institutional landscapes, corporate headquarters, master plans, and urban regeneration projects. MSP works with city leaders, planners, and builders at a strategic level so as to advocate for the inclusion of the public landscape as a means to achieve environmental, economic, social, and environmental sustainability. MSP's work demonstrates a deep commitment to the urban landscape as it performs as the platform for sustainable cities that are healthy across all aspects, sectors, and domains of urban life.

With offices in the United Kingdom, the United States, and China, MSP is engaged in projects and consultation around the globe and has to date worked on projects in over 20 countries and four continents.

MAXWAN Architects + Urbanists | 48

Web: www.maxwan.nl
Add: 'Vertrekhal Oranjelijn', Benjamin Franklinstraat 509, 3029 AC Rotterdam, The Netherlands
Tel: +31 (0)10 415 2999

Maxwan Architects+Urbanists are based in Rotterdam, in the Netherlands. They are an international practice dedicated to contemporary architectural and urban design. MAXWAN encourages collaboration between clients, colleagues, and specialist consultants. In each project, MAXWAN seek to merge cultural, technical, and aesthetic influences into an inextricable and beautiful whole. Considered among the most important offices to emerge from the Netherlands in the last ten years, MAXWAN have distinguished themselves as architects who design innovative urban town plans and as urban planners who make beautiful, intriguing buildings.

MAXWAN has a core staff of 15 designers and team leaders charged with five to ten young talents of various design professions. They collaborate with consultants in sustainability, building engineering, structural design, cost management, civil engineering, process management, and traffic flows.

Place Design Group | 34

Web: www.placedesigngroup.com
Add: 131 Robertson Street, Fortitude Valley , QLD 4006, Australia

Place Design Group has offices across Australia, China, and South East Asia. Integrating local knowledge with an international perspective, their team of over 200 bring together a myriad of ideas and trends to provide innovative solutions that transcend national boundaries.

Rehwaldt Landscape Architects | 148

Web: www.rehwaldt.de
Add: Bautzner Strasse 133, D - 01099 Dresden, Germany
Tel: +49 351 8119690

Rehwaldt Landscape Architects was founded in 1993 by Till Rehwaldt in Dresden. An analytical approach, based on intensive involvement with the local conditions, is the practice's main operating principal. This method is the guideline for their work, and they have developed parks, gardens, landscapes, and urban open spaces in very different spatial settings. They pursue the realization of conceptual ideas in all stages of a project—from the first sketch to the implementation of small details.

Strootman Landschapsarchitecten | 170, 212

Web: www.strootman.net
Add: Funenpark 1-D, 1019AK Amsterdam, The Netherlands
Tel: +31 20 419 41 69

Strootman Landschapsarchitecten is an award-winning office for landscape architecture and urban design. The work of Strootman integrates urbanism, cultural history, ecology, art, and architecture within a landscape architectural framework. This work takes the office from regional plans to garden design, from rural areas to the city, and from research to implementation.

A mix of analytical depth and design flair characterizes the work of Strootman; the team works meticulously through the analytical and conceptual stages, and then artistically develops the design scheme. The office combines thought with material craftsmanship, and strives for a certain earthy quality, warmth, and playfulness. The distinguishing feature of the work is the overarching sense of the natural and the earthy: the user becomes immersed in the spatial, visual, and temporal aspects of the landscape, true to the genius of the place but without the work losing a distinct design sensibility.

Sturt Noble Associates | 76, 126

Web: www.sturtassociates.com.au
Add: Suite 91,330 Wattle Street, Ultimo, NSW 2007, Australia
Tel: (61 2) 9211 3744

This multi-disciplinary team, with qualifications and expertise in landscape architecture, architecture, environmental planning and design, urban design, and horticulture, provides a personalized consultancy for a broad client base, including community, corporate, public, private, and institutional clients.

Sustainable solutions are fundamental to their practice and integrated into projects. Informed and inspired by natural and cultural landscapes, they work in collaboration with clients to generate solutions that combine creativity, sustainability, and cost-effectiveness.

Since 1990 their innovative and experienced teams in Sydney and Melbourne have enjoyed the opportunity to provide clients with professional expertise and exemplary service.

TERRITOIRES Landscape Architects | 188

Web: www.territoirespaysagistes.com
Add: 22, rue Mégevand, 25000 Besançon, France
Tel: 0033 (0)3 81 82 06 66

TERRITOIRES is a landscape architecture agency located in France and Switzerland. Their skillset is two-fold: landscape design and green engineering. The agency recently celebrated its 20th birthday. At the head of the company, Philippe Convercey (Conception), Franck Mathé (Production) and Etienne Voirot (Studies and Development) manage a team of ten, with technical, architectural/design, and communication expertise. By avoiding landscape stereotypes, they think outside the box and stay focused on the real needs of a place, aiming for the best possible use. Their design touch is as much radical in its aesthetics than it is functional and intelligible. Sustainable development and ecology are essential components of their planning. TERRITOIRES's work, visible in European public spaces, is saluted by numerous prizes. They are members of Swiss and French Landscape Architects Federations.

Topiaris Landscape Architecture | 68, 84

Web: www.topiaris.com
Tel: + 351 213 602 530
Fax: + 351 213 602 530

Topiaris is a landscape architecture firm founded in 1986 by four colleagues from the Technical University of Lisbon. Of this original group of partners, Teresa Barão and Luís Ribeiro remain, and were joined by Catarina Viana in 1995. In over two decades, Topiaris has sustained significant but steady growth while completing a considerable and significant number of projects in Portugal, with a well-established international presence, particularly in Angola and Cape Verde, and is currently setting up partnerships to extend its operational scope to Mozambique, East Timor, Algeria, and various countries across Central and Eastern Europe.

URBICUS Ltd | 98, 180, 228

Web: www.urbicus.fr
Add: 3 rue Edme Frémy, 78000 Versailles, France
Tel: +33 1 39494623

URBICUS has carried out all kinds of projects for regional developments at various locations since it was founded by Jean-Marc Gaulier in 1996. The agency works to transform landscapes whose public or private organizations entrust the work to them. URBICUS (in Latin 'of the city'), experiment with the consequences of civility projected in nature and nature, projected in towns. As town planners, architects, and landscape architects, they approach the landscape as a relevant way of tackling urban issues.

Published in Australia in 2015 by
The Images Publishing Group Pty Ltd
ABN 89 059 734 431
6 Bastow Place, Mulgrave, Victoria 3170, Australia
Tel: +61 3 9561 5544 Fax: +61 3 9561 4860
books@imagespublishing.com
www.imagespublishing.com

The Images Publishing Group Reference Number: 1203

Title: Country Parks
Author: Edited by Luis Paulo Faria Ribeiro
ISBN: 9781864706437

For Catalogue-in-Publication data, please see the National Library of Australia entry

Coordinated, edited and designed by Images Publishing, Shanghai (China) office.

Printed by Toppan Leefung Printing (Shenzhen) Co. Ltd / China